PARADE WITH BANNERS

PARADE

WITH

BANNERS

by *Donald Culross Peattie*

THE WORLD PUBLISHING COMPANY

Cleveland and New York

Published *by* THE WORLD PUBLISHING COMPANY

2231 WEST 110TH STREET, CLEVELAND 2, OHIO

Published *simultaneously in Canada by*

NELSON, FOSTER & SCOTT LTD.

Library of Congress Catalog Card Number: 57-10934

FIRST EDITION

Acknowledgments

For more than twenty years it has been the author's privilege to be invited to appear in the pages of *The Reader's Digest*, both in its domestic and its many foreign editions. Through no other medium could it have been possible for him to carry abroad so widely the stories of the American spirit which this book is intended to celebrate. As title to the articles which it has published rests with *The Reader's Digest*, it is with particular gratitude that acknowledgment is made of permission to reprint here, in part or wholly, chapters which originally appeared in *The Reader's Digest* as follows:

The Declaration of Independence	(July 1948)
Your Bill of Rights	(June 1947)
The Stars and Stripes	(April 1948)
I Like Uncle Sam's Bird	(January 1946)
Road Map to Adventure	(July 1950)
Rocky Mountain Roving	(June 1953)
Father Serra's Rosary	(May 1945)
Two Sights in the U. S. Never Forgotten	(August 1946)
California's Mother Lode	(November 1954)
Lee's Greatest Victory	(March 1950)
The White House	(November 1944)

ACKNOWLEDGMENTS

The Capitol: Constitution in Stone	(January 1953)
Grand Canyon	(April 1951)
The Washington Monument	(February 1945)
Arlington: Where Sleep the Brave	(August 1952)

The chapter Washington: Your Capital was written for *The Reader's Digest.* The sources of other chapters in this book are given below with cordial thanks to the editors for their permission to reprint them here:

Old Glory Takes to Sea	(*Country Gentleman,* January, 1951)
The Library that Thinks	(*Good Housekeeping,* February 1946, also *Scholastic Magazine,* April 22, 1946)
Tracks West	(*The Saturday Evening Post,* November 5, 1949)
The Ballad of Cynthia Ann	(*American Heritage,* April 1956)
The Spark on the Anvil	(*Westways,* January 1950)

By arrangement with *The Reader's Digest,* I Like Uncle Sam's Bird was also published in *Nature Magazine,* January 1946, Father Serra's Rosary thus appeared in *Catholic World,* May 1945, and The Washington Monument in *The Kiwanis Magazine,* February 1945. Acknowledgment of this is here cordially made.

Contents

CONTENTS

Dear Mark, my son:

These pages are an answer to your letter, the open answer for which you have called upon me with confidence that any father would try, at least, to meet. But for years now you have stood taller than I, journeyed farther, and better served the country of which you are now proud to be a modest representative. I cannot come up to your challenge —nor can I turn away from it.

That letter here on my desk—borne to me by stamps picturing royal elephants, pointed pagodas, delicate angular dancers—comes from a land so ancient, a nation so newly framed that it strikes one at first as a country of amusing fairy tale. You write of the fiery golden sunsets flaming behind silver-sheeted palaces, of a lovable people indolent in endless heat, of saffron-robed bonzes, lizards covering the ceiling, mold on your clothes from the tropical down-pours, and of ruined temples where Khmer heads of stone have smiled with inscrutable serenity for more than a thousand years upon jungle not long ago cleared to reveal them. You are at home now in that distant little kingdom, you and the gallant girl you married on her twenty-first birthday (which was my fifty-seventh). To me it is so far away I prefer to reckon the distance in terms of the days it takes to bring me word from you.

And yet this letter of yours from Cambodia comes, I

9

see, from the heart of the world. At least, I like to believe that nowhere does the world's heart beat more strongly than in our American desire for free brotherhood among peoples. To forward that is your job, "to go on calmly explaining our position to the Cambodian people," you write, "setting the record straight for them, helping maintain Cambodia's freedom, independence, and even—if it prefers it that way—its neutrality. I have never been so happy and tired in my work."

And I, in paternal satisfaction, might have rested on that, had you let me. But you go on—combining your young dignity as an officer of the United States Information Service with the fervor heard when you yelled for the Stanford Indians—"Yet I sometimes think in moments of despair that the world is going to pot, after all. Everywhere there is violence, gnawing away at the roots of world dignity and decency by those who preach doubt, disbelief, and treachery. In this battle for ideas we need every gun we've got. The bigger the better, because the other side is not playing for peanuts. I am convinced more than ever out here that this battle for men's minds will be decisive in the next twenty or perhaps even fifteen years. To win it we have to get people at home thinking more about the fight, showing them the goals at stake, and why we must care. For this, Father, you must do what you can. Surely there's enough great American history to help you do it."

Well, a loyal son always rates his father's powers too highly. But you are right, Mark, about the power of American history (the subject of your strenuous student years), to say nothing of the evocative power of our country's finest institutions, its great men and monuments, its shrines and symbols, and the very glory of its natural sweep from coast to thundering coast. To these things, and what I have said of them in one or another forum, I turn in answer to your demand. I do not pretend that I fulfill it, or ever could. But I remember your last words, at the airport where the great glittering plane stood waiting to carry you and your bride Alice out toward the Far East. You smiled as you said them, kissing your mother good-by. "Keep the flags flying, Mother!" you said, and left us.

In these pages I have tried to raise for you—for all of us and for any far away who may catch sight of their flutter —a few of our American banners.

Your
Father

PARADE WITH BANNERS

The Declaration of
Independence—America's
Gospel

When I speak to my friends about the adventure on which
you and Alice are embarked, out there in Southeast Asia,
I find that all that most of them know of the United States
Information Agency (or Service, as you call it overseas)
is just the Voice of America. You'll want me to tell of
more than that, though the Voice is a great story in itself.
It broadcasts "around the clock, around the globe," as they
tell it, in forty-one languages, penetrating the Bamboo
Curtain and the Iron Curtain so effectively that its enemies
work desperately to "jam" it. Indeed, the men at USIA
in Washington estimate that the Communists spend four
times as much money in that attempt as we spend on
the whole world-wide operations of the Voice. For a taste

of the truth makes men hunger for it, and, starved on lies, they spit them out and risk their skins for what the short waves bring them.

In friendlier lands, and in the uncommitted countries, USIS works not only in thin air, but from solid footholds. Its posts and outposts number over two hundred, in some seventy-eight nations, from Iceland to Nigeria, from Laos to Afghanistan. Newspapers, magazines, motion-picture films, television broadcasts, pamphlets and posters, libraries and lectures flow from the expert hands of USIS personnel. These men are trained as you, my son, were trained those weeks in Washington, with Alice learning, too, how rightly to represent this country overseas. Thus USIA is as much a branch of our defense as Army, Navy, and Air Force. Or so the President says.

It's a grand sight when any detachment of our armed services goes by, flag high and footsteps ringing to some brassy march. You and your fellows in the USIS personnel scattered around the world can't fall in behind them, nor do you want to. It's the straight thinking and the high beliefs and the free spirit of our country at its best that you want the multitudes of other peoples to behold. And surely, at the head of any such parade, must come the prime standard of the nation.

T O EVERY ardent American, the proclamation of our nation's creed, made at its birth, sounds as fresh as though the ink were still wet upon the words.

"We hold these truths to be self-evident, that all men are created equal . . ."

This is young Thomas Jefferson, drafting a *Declaration by the Repesentatives of the* UNITED STATES OF AMERICA *in General Congress Assembled.* He, so gifted and so privileged, did not deceive himself that men are alike, but, profoundly spiritual in his democracy, he knew that they were equal before God. So the pen flowed on surely, "—that they are endowed by their Creator with certain inalienable rights; that among these are life, liberty and the pursuit of happiness . . ."

Thomas Jefferson had read his Locke, the English philosopher, who spoke of "life, liberty and property." Mr. Jefferson of "Monticello," had property himself, but he knew that not for property do men go to war, and stop bullets with their hearts. In the past year Americans had died, at Lexington and Bunker Hill, for certain inalienable rights which could and should be within the reach of all.

"—that to secure these rights," the pen therefore wrote, "governments are instituted among men, deriving their just powers from the consent of the governed . . ." The bells of Philadelphia chimed the hours, as the gospel of this nation took form. But one bell did not yet ring. Silent on its moldering beams in the cupola of the Pennsylvania State House, it commanded prophetically in words from Leviticus encircling its crown: *Proclaim liberty throughout all the land and unto all the inhabitants thereof.*

Thomas Jefferson wrote the first draft of the Declaration of Independence in two days. He never claimed that its ideas were original with him; his task was to express the thought of all Americans, not one American. Not only had patriots, from Savannah to Portsmouth, been saying such things for some fifty years, but the rights they were here demanding were the same that Englishmen had fought for these last five centuries. And the theory of democratic government here announced was in the greatest English tradition of Milton and Locke and the judicial decisions of Sir Edward Coke. Such thoughts, transplanted to America, had grown like noble trees, in the deeds and words of Roger Williams and William Penn.

That the time had come for American independence had been proved to the simplest understanding by Tom Paine's "Common Sense," a pamphlet published only six months earlier, but passed from hand to hand in every town. The denunciations of George the Third's misrule, which follow each other in the Declaration like a hail of bullets, were taken almost word for word from the preamble to the Virginia Constitution—written short weeks ago by Jefferson himself! And on June 7, only three days before Jefferson set to work on the Declaration, fiery Richard Henry Lee of Virginia, though his family was in

England, hostage to fortune, had moved in Congress: "*Resolved*, that these United Colonies are, and of a right ought to be, free and independent States, that they are absolved from all allegiance to the British Crown, and that all political connection, between them and the State of Great Britain is, and ought to be totally dissolved."

Almost those very words are, and of a right ought to be, found in the Declaration. For though the conservatives had forced a postponement of debate on Lee's all-out Resolution, if it was passed it would constitute the act, and fact, of independence. And Jefferson's Declaration was to be the explanation, to the world, of this act.

When Jefferson had finished his rough draft he took it around to his fellow committeemen, chiefly John Adams and Benjamin Franklin (confined to his room with gout). Some of their changes are known, because they made them in their own hands on the manuscript of the first draft. But not a paragraph nor an idea did they add or drop; all they did was to point up a phrase here, subdue a bit of young Jefferson's runaway rhetoric there.

On June 28, the committee's draft of the Declaration was presented to Congress, which set it momentarily aside till Lee's Resolution should be acted on. Debate for that was scheduled for July 1, and that day dawned sizzling hot. As Congress convenes in the State House at nine o'clock, the stately room is crowded with the delegates already mopping their brows, uncomfortable in those stiff coats of sky blue and cherry red, primrose yellow and peach pink. But there is nothing gay about the delegates themselves as they clash in bitter debate, led by fiery John

Adams of Massachusetts pitted against obstinate conserva-
tive John Dickinson of Pennsylvania. As they argue, the
British fleet bringing Lord Howe's Redcoats and Hessian
mercenaries is sighted off Sandy Hook, and in New York
George Washington starts a messenger galloping towards
Philadelphia.

Easy to ask now why any delegate patriotic enough to
have been sent by his colony to Congress would oppose
independence. The men who, like Dickinson, voted against
it to the last called themselves "olive-branch men"—ap-
peasers, in the language of today. Or they thought you
could still do business with George the Third. They were
the kind who say: Don't split the country now by trying
to decide our war aims. Let's win the war first, and an-
nounce ideals (if any) afterwards. They were like the people
who think you can't defend democracy abroad because it
isn't perfect at home. Some claimed to represent interests
too important to be risked for moral sentiments—banking,
big shipping and importing firms, slave-owning planters of
wealth.

And who were the fifty-six we call the Signers? They
were typical Americans precisely because you can't type
them. They were a mixture of native-born and foreign-born,
rich and poor, farmers and inventors, financiers and physi-
cians, self-made and to-the-manor-born. They had little
book learning or were college graduates; they were Protestants or Catholics or freethinkers. But something they all
had in common: they were their brother's keepers; they
put the public business before their private interests; they

knew that you cannot let liberty be taken from your neighbor without losing it yourself.

As the debate mounted in bitterness, the July day boiled up to a thunderstorm that crashed above the city waiting tensely for news from these secret deliberations. The slumbering bell in the loft thrummed in answer to peals of thunder. When the storm passed the sun was sinking in a clear gold west and even the opposition knew that Mr. Adams and "the radicals" had won. The disgruntled objectors were being persuaded to stay away on the morrow when the vote would be taken. But Delaware's vote was tied, George Read against, Thomas M'Kean for Independence; her third delegate, Caesar Rodney, was with his own people fighting a Tory uprising in his home state. M'Kean sent a rider dashing southward through the night to bring him back. And ever nearer was galloping the weary messenger from General Washington.

The second of July was gray and cool—the very mood for taking a momentous resolve. The new delegates sent by New Jersey arrived and demanded to hear the arguments all over, and at this juncture came the news from George Washington. At that, men and Colonies which had been doubtful fell into line. Then, just before the voting started, in dashed Caesar Rodney, mud-spattered after a ride of eighty miles without stopping, in time to break the deadlock in his delegation and make unanimous the vote of the thirteen united colonies for the Resolution for Independence.

"The second day of July 1776," wrote John Adams, "will

be the most memorable . . . in the history of America. I . . . believe that it will be celebrated by succeeding generations as the great anniversary festival. It ought to be commemorated . . . with Pomp and Parade, with Shows, Games, Sports, Guns, Bells, Bonfires and Illuminations from one end of this continent to the other from this time forward forever. . . . You will think me transported with enthusiasm, but I am not. I am well aware of the toil and blood and treasure that it will cost us to maintain this Declaration, and support and defend these States—yet through all the gloom I can see the rays of ravishing Light and Glory."

Debate on Jefferson's Declaration started on July 3, with the weather clear and fine and a brisk wind blowing away the cobwebs of yesterday's fatigues. Congress formed itself into a committee of the whole—that is, all the members became critics and revisers and fellow draftsmen of the Declaration, without the hobbling of parliamentary rules. Though Jefferson fumed silently at the changes made, while kindly old Ben Franklin calmed him with philosophical observations and funny anecdotes, a comparison of his draft with the final document shows that most of the corrections were on the side of accuracy, clarity, and a sharpening of the points. Miraculously, fifty-six cooks improved the broth! Their most important deletion was Jefferson's passionate demand for the abolition of slavery. The men freeing our country could not now settle that dark question; only by avoiding it could unanimity be obtained.

The fourth of July dawned fair and warmer, a glorious, cloudless summer day. Congress again resumed its formal parliamentary sittings and reported to itself what it had done yesterday as a committee of the whole. By four o'clock the final vote was taken, the delegates voting by colonies, not as individuals, and thus was the Declaration of Independence unanimously approved. The last act of Congress on that day was to order the Declaration to the printer, with copies to be sent out to all assemblies, conventions, congresses, councils of safety, and commanding officers of our forces in the field, in forts, and aboard our ships.

We are in the habit of speaking of the Fourth of July as the day when the Declaration of Independence was signed. But sober history informs us that nobody signed that day except John Hancock, President of Congress, who merely affixed his name as a token signature to make the document official. Yet we are right in celebrating the "Glorious Fourth," as the birth date of our nation. The Declaration announces itself to the world as "the Unanimous Declaration of the thirteen UNITED STATES OF AMERICA" —the first time that those last four momentous words were ever officially used. From that moment the colonies became the States, and the States were in the Union, which is older by a year than the Stars and Stripes, seven years older than the treaty of peace with Great Britain, and eleven years older than the framing of the Constitution.

All night of July 4-5, printer John Dunlap and his typesetters worked to set up the first broadsides, or handbills, of the Declaration and by the next morning they were on the streets, like "extra" papers today. The Pennsylvania *Evening Post* was the first (July 6) to publish it; then, as messengers galloped north and south, paper after paper reprinted it. It is odd to read these journals, without head-lines, without editorial comment, announcing the greatest event of the age. But they were snatched from hand to hand, read from the pulpits, and in the crossroads taverns. Down in South Carolina a thirteen-year-old boy named Andrew Jackson read it in a piping voice to backwoods patriots. Meantime, in Philadelphia, at exactly noon of July 8, John Nixon, a member of the Pennsylvania Committee of Safety, read the Declaration of Independence aloud from a wooden platform in what we now know as Independence Square, to a great concourse of people. Battalions of soldiers fired salutes, and across the city bell shouted to bell. And now at last the great bell—the Liberty Bell—roused from its slumbers, and from its deep throat proclaimed liberty unto all the land and to the inhabitants thereof.

On July 9, George Washington ordered his brigades into hollow squares, on the spot where New York's City Hall now stands, and had the Declaration read aloud "in a clear voice" by one of his aides—and so small was his army facing all the might of Britain, that it was heard by the last recruit. On July 18, Boston went wild with joy, and thirteen cannons fired salvo after salvo; bells were rung till they rocked their steeples, every ship in the harbor fired salutes and the guns in forts and batteries bellowed. So the glad tidings sped—at a snail's pace, as it seems now, but incredibly fast then—until on August 10 far-off Savannah greeted independence with fireworks and buried King George in effigy with a mock funeral.

Few of us realize that the real date of the signing of the Declaration of Independence was a hot and ominous day in August—the second. The document which Congress assembled on that date to sign was an "engrossed copy," that is, a copy in beautiful penmanship by Timothy Matlock, who had also engrossed George Washington's commission as Commander in Chief. Matlock inscribed the entire Declaration on a single sheet, and this is the copy, enshrined in the Archives Building, which we call "the" Declaration of Independence.

But to sign this document was now far more dangerous than when Congress voted to adopt the Declaration on July the Fourth. The war had taken a turn for the worse; Washington was outnumbered four to one, another enemy force was gathering in Canada, and the encouraged American Tories were adding civil war to invasion from across the seas. The men who signed now would have to fulfill to the letter the brave words with which the Declaration closes—that to the cause of independence they pledged "their lives, their fortunes, and their sacred honor." All were putting their heads in the noose reserved for condemned traitors. They knew it, too. When Hancock said, "We must all hang together," Franklin quipped, "If we don't we shall all hang separately." Fat Benjamin Harrison chaffed skinny Elbridge Gerry, "It will be all over with me in a minute, but you will be kicking in the air half an hour after I'm gone." Tradition has it that as John Hancock signed his name with a great flourish he said, "There, King George can read that without spectacles." Actually he never put his "John Hancock" on any document without a flourish— he was a flourishing sort of man. As Croesus-rich Carroll of Carrollton signed, one member whispered, "There goes a million." John Adams scanned the face of every Signer from Josiah Bartlett, the first to sign as he had been the first to vote for the Declaration, to the last, grim Abraham Clark of New Jersey. Some might be lukewarm, Adams thought, some reluctant upon principle. But if anyone felt fear, Adams proudly states, he could not tell it from their graven masks.

More, some who had earlier voted contrary had now courageously changed their minds. Some who for months had fought for Lee's Resolution and Jefferson's Declaration were absent on military duty at this time and did not have the opportunity to sign their names until months later. Some who were not even members of Congress in July and had been elected since, were permitted, because of their known patriotism, to affix their signatures to the document and thus become immortal.

The Declaration fulfilled the fondest hopes for it. Thus when Lord Howe's army seemed about to capture Philadelphia, "Nothing but the signing and recognizing of the Declaration of Independence," wrote Signer and Congressman Benjamin Rush, "preserved the Congress from dissolution." The Declaration was vital in the diplomacy of securing the French alliance. It unified the country, and divided the enemy.

The immortal document not only made history, but has had a history of its own. Thrice it has fled for its life; first when Congress evacuated Philadelphia after the defeats at Brandywine and Germantown, again when in 1814 the British captured and burned Washington. Legend has it that Dolly Madison saved it, but history shows that General Pleasonton hastily removed it from the State Department to Leesburg, Virginia. When in 1941 Japan and Germany declared war the Declaration was once more feared in danger, in an age of long-range bombing, and was buried in the vaults at Fort Knox, Kentucky. Today it is the most sacred relic, save only the Constitution itself, in the possession of the nation.

The ink of the document and the fifty-six immortal signatures has faded. The grievances enumerated against George the Third have faded out no less. But the great body of human rights announced in the preamble lives on, and is more precious and needed today than on July Fourth, 1776. For in other parts of the world tyranny is even stronger now than it was then. Freedom is ours, but the Declaration reminds us that it should belong to *all* men. To forward it, we must see to it that in our own country, in each of our states, in our home town, our own street, in our very hearts, we fulfill towards our neighbors the spirit and the letter of that deathless document.

Your Bill of Rights

Here in my pleasant house in my California garden, far from such discomforts as give Phnom Penh the rank of "hardship post," I feel abashed yet pleased to have you write, "You're on the front lines, Father, out here with me," just because some of my books are on the "American Bookshelf" that USIS distributes. Who would not feel a tingle at being asked to yield translation rights for any tongues among the following: Arabic, Assamese, Bengali, Bicol, Burmese, Cambodian, Cebuano, Chinese, Danish, Dutch, Farsi, Finnish, Greek, Gujarati, Hebrew, Hiligaynon, Hindi, Hungarian, Icelandic, Ilocano, Indonesian, Japanese, Kachin, Kannada, Korean, Laotian, Macedonian, Malay, Malayalam, Marathi, Norwegian, Oriya, Polish, Portuguese, Punjabi, Romanian, Serbo-Croatian, Sindhi, Sinhalese, Slovenian, Spanish, Swedish, Tagalog, Tamil, Telegu, Thai, Turkish, Urdu, Vietnamese.

I haven't a notion where some of those lingoes are talked, nor can I always recognize the alphabets in which these *books of mine are printed, when copies are sent, with official courtesy, to join the legible ones on my shelves. I only hope that something of what I have said in them may interest some splendid Ghashgai horseman of the Persian plains, or some philosophic lama in a Tibetan monastery. But my hope is humble.*

To tell your own countrymen about what is to them unconsciously the very breath of daily life is a challenge of a different sort, a less recondite honor. Or so I felt when asked by my magazine, The Reader's Digest, to do an article about our Bill of Rights. For that I went to Washington, not just to see the noble document in the original, but to be set straight on certain meanings of it by men who knew them best, like the Attorney General of the United States, and Justices I knew, of the Supreme Court. I was thankful that I had had such guidance for my unsure hand, when the little piece was printed in pamphlet form and distributed (the only "literature" so offered) from the Freedom Train. It was in the fall of 1947 that our government sent out the Train to tour the country, bearing not only the great original Bill, but a hundred and fifty other sacred documents of American history. A sort of USIS program for our own citizenry—and who can deny that most among us need it?

THE most significant piece of paper in your life and mine and that of every American is enshrined in the Library of Congress* in Washington. It is the original document that promises us, in ink that has faded in more than a century and a half but in words that never dim, most of what we mean by our "Constitutional rights."

Yet few of those rights are found in the Constitution as originally drawn. They are to be sought, rather, in the first ten amendments to the Constitution, passed by Congress in 1791. The single great sheet—great in every sense—that bears on its yellowing face these precious liberties is called the Bill of Rights. And it means more to the American citizen than the Constitution itself, which is the draft—marvelously farsighted, clear, and stable—for our governmental machinery, signed in 1787 by our Founding Fathers. You might, for instance, change the way by which, under the original Consitution, senators are elected (indeed it's been done) without causing the national blood pressure to jump. But lay one finger on Article I of the Bill of Rights, which protects freedom of utterance, and every good American—though the utterance be his bitterest opponent's—should be up in arms.

It's the same with the other nine amendments; take away

* Now in the Archives Building.

one and you weaken all; take freedom from your neighbor and you enslave yourself. "Liberty," said the late beloved William Allen White, Main Street's most famous editor, "is the only thing you cannot have unless you are willing to give it to others."

So, to Americans, the first ten amendments have the force of moral law, on a higher plane than ordinary legislation. As they are our fundamental articles of faith, they cannot be abridged or abolished even by Congress, for they are part of the compact between all citizens. Thus they are the supreme law of the land, and we set the Supreme Court to prowl around the liberties they promise, and to fling to earth any laws that would lessen their force. Yet, marvelous to relate, they are not written in lawyer language. Anybody can understand the Bill of Rights, just as anybody can understand the Ten Commandments: "Thou shalt not kill. Thou shalt not steal."

Only the Ten Commandments manage to say so much in so little. Take grand old Article I which sets forth in one sentence enough freedoms to make dictatorship impossible in this country as long as Americans give unto their neighbors that which they would have themselves:

> "Congress shall make no law respecting an establishment of religion, or prohibiting the free exercize thereof; or abridging the freedom of speech, or of the Press; or the right of the people peaceably to assemble, and to petition the Government for redress of grievances."

There, in one breath and at the outset of its history, a government took the unprecedented step of protecting the citizens against itself. It freed religion from all interference by the state and, not less importantly, made it impossible for any sect to seize the reins of government. By promising free speech and press, this government exposed itself, as no dictatorship dares for one moment to do, to the bracing winds of open criticism.

So you may with impunity criticise and roundly denounce Congress, the President, even the decisions of the Supreme Court, providing you do not slander or libel individual persons. One hardly knows what to admire more in this freedom of utterance—the psychological wisdom of providing a safety valve for the pressures that inevitably build up in a complex society, or the way such freedom operates to keep government on its toes.

True that other countries, too, permit freedom of speech and press, as well as most or all of our other rights in these immortal amendments. But in other countries they are usually found in tradition, precedent, common law, or some special enactment. Our government was the first to collect them all in one place and write them into its very Constitution and so set them where they could be seen by all, denied by none. As a result, the Bill of Rights is in the very blood of our people; even those who may never have read the document are as familiar with the outlines of each of its freedoms as they are with the features of George Washington or Abraham Lincoln.

No confiscation of your property by the government, says the Bill of Rights, unless you are indemnified for it or have forfeited your right to it by just laws; no entering of your houses, without swearing out of a warrant, to search your papers; no accusations by witnesses unless they can be produced in open court; no putting you on trial twice for the same accusation. The Bill of Rights promises you freedom from excessive bail, freedom from torture to obtain confessions, freedom from cruel and unusual punishment. It gives you the right to form a militia, to a speedy trial by jury, to a definite written accusation if you are tried, and to have counsel and subpoena witnesses in a criminal trial. So, as long as we relax no vigilance, you and I and all of us are the freest and politically the safest people on earth.

But we didn't get our Bill of Rights because some high-minded gentlemen penned easy, self-evident truths so long ago. The amendments were not conceived and brought to birth merely because needed and desired, any more than a child is. Our democratic liberty was conceived ages ago in the dark of dungeons where brave mind whispered to unbroken soul. It was wrenched into birth when limbs were pulled apart on the torturer's rack, and knew the screams of women who saw their men butchered. It drew its breath of life as the ill-trained farm boys choked their last, pinned to the earth on Brooklyn Heights by the bayonets of Hessian mercenaries. For man's belief that he has "natural rights" or "God-given rights" is far older than the American nation that is founded on it. It is so old you cannot find its beginning.

And the fight to gain recognition of these "inalienable rights" is as old as man's faith in them. Tyranny is a sleepless foe. Always somewhere in the world men are being told they have no rights but what the State allows them. Such a State tells you what happiness to pursue. It gives you but one liberty—to obey. Answerable to nobody, it takes your property or your life as it pleases. Call this feudalism, despotism, State-ism, or some current-ism; it is always the some old enemy, and knows it cannot live in the world with our philosophy, that "governments derive their just powers from the consent of the governed."

The limitations on the power of government which we have defined in the Bill of Rights are foreshadowed in earliest laws and morals. Some are suggested by Magna Carta. Some are written into the Roman code which maintained the essential dignity of the free citizen however poor, and the sanctity of woman's person. Some are implicit in the teachings of Christ which set human values above property values and protect the humble against the proud. Over and over the Old Testament tells us that all men are created equal—not alike, naturally, but equal in the sight of a just God before whom kings stand naked as their slaves.

So that the ancestry of the Bill of Rights lies in the noblest thoughts of men, though its American mother is our Declaration of Independence. But actually the American people had been hammering away at the problems of democratic self-government for one hundred and fifty years before our revolution reached the shooting stage. Rocking on the wild Atlantic, the *Mayflower* Pilgrims in 1620 drew up, in their famous Compact, the first instrument of our democracy—inadequate, imperfect, but an honest beginning. The primary mistakes of the Puritans were corrected by Roger Williams' statement of religious freedom in 1644. In 1682 William Penn wrested from the English king his

marvelous Charter of Liberties for Pennsylvania. The words
"inalienable natural rights" turn up in a petition signed by
the inhabitants of Anson County, North Carolina, in
1769. The Virginia Bill of Rights (1776) and the Massachusetts Bill of Rights (1780) were but the elder sisters of
the first ten amendments to the Constitution.

No wonder that, when the Founding Fathers signed a
Constitution that enumerated only a few rights of the common citizen, the people were indignant. They had not
fought a bloody war, ill-armed, starving, barefoot, set on
by regiments of brutal mercenaries, by Indians, and by
Tories, in order merely to get a President, however good,
or elect a Senate. With their feet planted on the Declaration of Independence they had fought, and died, and won,
in order to secure their individual liberties, their *rights*.
And they knew what they meant by these.

So did some of the delegates to the Constitutional Convention, who refused to sign the original document because
it contained no Bill of Rights. So did Thomas Jefferson,
who wrote from Paris (where he was ambassador when the
Constitution was signed) indignant protest at this crying
lack. Some of the states only ratified the Constitution on
the understanding that a Bill of Rights would be added.

In this first inaugural address, George Washington re-
minded Congress of this duty. That is how, on June 8, 1789,
James Madison came to present nine amendments to the
Senate. They drew largely on the earlier Virginia Bill of
Rights authored by that great democratic-aristocrat, George
Mason, one of Washington's near neighbors on the
Potomac, and on Madison's own work for religious free-

dom in Virginia. In the House, seventeen amendments were offered. Eventually House and Senate agreed on twelve, but the states failed to ratify the first two that you will see on the original document. So the remaining ten amendments became the law of the land, as Jefferson, in his capacity of Secretary of State, was proud to inform the governors of the States on March 1, 1792.

Thus you got your Bill of Rights. Sometimes you hear that it "guarantees" you your liberties. I asked the then Attorney General of the United States about that word, as we stood examining the grand old document before it started on its country-wide tour, on the Freedom Train. That night I asked one of the Supreme Court justices, as we sat in his home only a few miles from Gunston Hall, George Mason's mansion. Both gave the same answer: The Bill of Rights *promises* much, but it is up to the American people to make that promise good.

Even the Attorney General cannot stop men from dressing up in bed sheets and horsewhipping fellow citizens for trying to vote under the Fifteenth Amendment; he can only punish these homemade fascists, providing people who know them are brave enough to testify against them. Even the Supreme Court cannot prevent the so-called "nullification laws" passed by anti-integration states; it can only slap down such legislation after it has reared its head. The Bill of Rights is just as effective in preventing abuses as you and I make it. There are no infractions of it that are "no concern of mine."

And there is no year, perhaps no month or day, that the Bill of Rights is not violated in some way, somewhere. Its most dangerous foes are not now foreign dictators but those of us who, while claiming every privilege of democratic liberty, would deny it to others. To rise to a neighbor's aid in defense of his rights is a first duty of citizenship. A second is outspoken criticism of every form of local and federal government when it fails in its duty to the first ten amendments. When the people *think*, and say what they think, this government obeys.

Those ten amendments are only Page One of the Bill of Rights. For that document was not completed when ratified in 1791. It still left millions of souls born under the American flag with no more rights than pigs or dogs, for they were slaves, chattels of their masters. It took a war and the Thirteenth, Fourteenth and Fifteenth Amendments to give other races the promise of freedom, citizenship, and the right to vote. But even in 1865 the fight was not over. One half the adult population was still disenfranchised. It took the Nineteenth Amendment to give the vote to women. These amendments to the Bill of Rights were further steps along the road of American evolution.

No one can say what the next amendment will be. But in guarding its Bill of Rights the American public cannot afford to sleep. It cannot safely delegate to anyone, no matter how noble a leader, the business of being night watchman of its most precious treasure. Not thus were bought the great liberties of the Bill of Rights. They were paid for in agony and blood, and can be kept safe only by restless conscience and the courage to speak out.

The Stars and Stripes

You have from childhood, Mark, been fascinated by flags. So are many small boys, but their interest usually wanes as they grow and begin to think the busier thoughts of adulthood. With you—just the opposite. I brought you home a flag of the tiny republic, the oldest in the world, of San Marino, and you flew it on your battered car at college all year long. Now you return the compliment. You send me the flag of Cambodia, which shows, between stripes of blue on a broad red field, a conventionalized design in white of three-towered Angkor Wat.

This is a new flag upon the winds of the world, new not because Cambodia is new—it is one of the oldest nations on earth—but because national banners are new. The Roman Empire, through its long history, never had a flag—just those poles surmounted by the fierce golden eagles and the device, S.P.Q.R. Even the empire of Genghis Khan, which stretched from Russia to Korea, from India to the Arctic Ocean, had only the traditional Mongol insignia—a bunch of yak tails dangling from a pole.

As late as the Middle Ages there were few truly national *banners. Many were but the coat of arms of the knight or king under whom professional soldiers fought. The old flag of France was a snowy white affair with golden* fleur-de-lis *sprinkled upon it—all as pretty as the coverlet for a queen's bed. The old English flag, before the Union Jack was devised, was a long gaudy streamer on which were quartered the king's arms: the Irish harp (quite against the will of the Irish!), the Scottish lion (rampant with indignation), and two quarters of three lions each—dachshund-shaped English beasts.*

The medieval guilds and many churchly orders carried gonfalons, not true flags. They consisted of lifeless standards hanging stiffly on a horizontal bar depending from a pole. Later, regiments might have their guidons (guides-hommes) —little pennants flown from lances.

But it takes a genuine feeling of nationality to create the true flag of a country and to keep it floating, rippling, and snapping on the winds of popular love. That is why Italy and Germany, both divided up into rival states till well past the middle of the last century, did not get national banners until long after an upstart country like the United States had created and honored one, and baptized it in blood and fire. Now in the wave of nationalism sweeping the world, every nation must needs have its flag.

A while ago, a citizen of the new Republic of India wrote me that though India now had a flag and many paid it lip service and gave it salutes, few seemed to have any deep, stirring emotions about it. He asked me what Americans, who hold their flag in such veneration, could suggest to make the Indian flag more beloved and genuinely respected in Indian hearts.

I had to answer that India, old as it is, would have to live with its flag through a lot more history. That our "star-sprinkled bunting" had only slowly gained ground in the hearts of the American people. And that a national flag is like a child—the more one sacrifices for it, the more beloved it becomes.

AT SUNSET, as the white light goes and the last red rays streak the sky, as the zenith blue darkens and the stars steal forth, our flag all over the world is saluted by the troops that guard it. This ceremony, called standing *Retreat*, is a custom that goes back farther than the memory of the oldest living veteran. One of the youngest, my son, told me: "Men who hate everything else in military life love standing *Retreat*. You're all in it together, company commander and private, as the last light leaves the sky. The company is brought to *Parade Rest*, the bugles call *To the Colors*, the band strikes up our anthem, and as the troops present arms and officers salute, the flag is lowered and caught in the color sergeant's hands so that it never touches the earth. To the rookie, *Retreat* may be the one uplifting moment in a day of grind and homesickness. But I've seen old Army men with tears in their eyes, as if they'd never before seen the flag come home for the night."

Over and over, as the old globe of earth turns toward night, men see our colors down with this loving dignity. One hour after the bright folds sink from the fading sky on the Atlantic seaboard, the standard in all Mississippi Valley posts is lowered. Two hours after that, bugles on the Pacific coast are calling *To the Colors*; in three hours more, the far-off notes float over Pearl Harbor. And as the spinning planet rolls into dawn, "tomorrow" is breaking on the farthest island outposts—Wake and Guam and Okinawa —and the Stars and Stripes are run up briskly to snap in the morning breeze. In triumph they float over Iwo Jima, where Lieutenant Harold G. Schrier of Richmond, Missouri, first planted them atop Mount Suribachi at 10:35 on the morning of February 23, 1945.

The Associated Press photographer who, at a second flag-raising on Mount Suribachi that day, caught those four Marines pushing up the pole while the banner lifted on the battle wind, snapped the most famous picture of World War II. It took our breath, and we all declared that the figures, grouped in a composition too vital to be posed, looked as if sculptured. Today a monument carefully based upon the photograph, made by sculptor Felix W. De Weldon, and cast in bronze, stands at the north end of Arlington National Cemetery, with a duplicate guarding the entrance to the Marine Corps Base at Quantico, Vir-

ginia. The monument and the photograph speak for themselves—and for all the men who have died for that flag
in the years between Iwo Jima and the day when, in 1777,
it was first flung on the winds of destiny.

Young as our nation is, our flag is today the eighth oldest
national emblem still in use, second in age only to the
Swiss among the republics of the world. True that there
are older American flags, exhibiting a variety of pines,
rattlesnakes, palms, moons, mottoes, or modifications of
the British banner; Washington himself, January 1, 1776,
raised a "Congress" flag having thirteen red and white
stripes and a miniature Union Jack in the canton (the
corner rectangle), and a Rhode Island regiment had a
white banner with thirteen stars in a blue canton.

All these may claim to be early American flags, since
Americans made and hoisted them. But not one of them is
the flag. Not one is the Stars and Stripes, the flag of the
United States, which, even as a living person, has a definite
birth date. And like a beloved personality, it has become
more precious with the years; like a faith long held, its
meaning has grown clearer and stronger. Borne high by
victory in the greatest of all wars, gripped securely by the
world's mightiest power, it is at this hour of history caught
by a new wind that blows to us from beyond our borders
and flutters the colors with new hope and challenge.

Who created it, this emblem so breath-taking in its
beauty, its stripes rippling like the sinews of a living body,
its stars flashing out in unison from the folds of midnight
blue? Legend, tradition, mythology, fiction shout their
answers. History is more cautious.

Familiar from our schoolbooks is the Betsy Ross legend, based on the fact that the widow Ross, upholsterer of Arch Street, Philadelphia, received from the state of Pennsylvania payment for having made some "ships' colors." Whatever they may have been, they were not the American flag, for this payment was dated *before* June 14, 1777, when Congress passed the following:

"Resolved, that the flag of the United States shall be thirteen stripes, alternate red and white; that the union shall be thirteen stars, white in a blue field, representing a new constellation." National recognition of this resolution as the official birth of our flag was fixed in our calendar in 1916 when President Wilson proclaimed June 14 to be, henceforth, Flag Day.

The final authority on the flag is Congress, since Congress fathered it. When Francis Hopkinson, a signer of the Declaration of Independence, suggested that Congress might appropriately send him a quarter cask of wine, for "having designed the flag of the United States," and later raised his price to "forty-five pounds in hard money," Congress answered that many others had played a part in making the flag, and rebuked Hopkinson for setting a price on his patriotic services. So credit goes to no one man or woman, but to Congress itself, the representatives of the American people. And that, surely, is a fitting place to leave the honors.

When in the War of 1812 a Washington lawyer named Francis Scott Key was detained on the ship *Minden* during the bombardment of Fort McHenry, near Baltimore, our star-spangled banner was given its voice. By the dawn's

early light of September 14, 1814, after British warships
had thrown some fifteen hundred shells and bombs into
Fort McHenry, lawyer Key could see that our flag was
still there. His poem was completed on shore soon after,
and sung, a short time later, under its glittering title. A
star-spangled buoy in Chesapeake Bay today marks the
approximate position of the *Minden*.

Few know that you can see the very flag we sing of, the
original star-spangled banner, in the Arts and Industries
Building of the National Museum, in Washington. Twenty-
nine feet high on the hoist, and thirty-two feet wide on the
fly, with fifteen,* not thirteen, red and white stripes, this
banner was designed and sewed by Mrs. Mary Pickersgill
of Baltimore and her thirteen-year-old daughter, Caroline.
Owing to its immense size, work on it dragged until the
defeat of our troops at Bladensburg, Maryland. Then,
laboring feverishly, the woman and the little girl completed
it just in time to present it to Fort McHenry before the
British fleet hove in sight.

The National Museum also has custody of the flag from
which our emblem takes its most loving nickname. This
banner was presented to seafaring William Driver of Salem,
Massachusetts, in 1824, and flew at the masthead of his
ship on two voyages around the world. "Old Glory" he
named it, and when he left the sea he took it with him to
Nashville, Tennessee, where he used to fly it on every
occasion. So it was already famous when war broke out

* From 1795 until 1818 the flag had fifteen stars, representing the
thirteen states, and the first two subsequent states, Vermont and
Kentucky, to join the Union.

between the states. The Texas Rangers searched his house for it repeatedly. Not till federal troops captured the city was it learned that the old seaman, plying his practiced needle, had sewed the flag up in his coverlet, and had been sleeping under it for months. When Captain Driver was allowed to raise "Old Glory" with his own hands over the state capitol, the fame of his flag swept over the country, and the words "Old Glory" were gradually transferred as a fitting name for every flag of the United States.

The war of the Blue and the Gray brought one flag the most terrific baptism of fire our colors had ever received. In April 1861 every Confederate battery in Charleston harbor rained shells on Fort Sumter, where Major Anderson with only sixty men kept the Stars and Stripes flying. The defiance of that flag drove the Charleston *Mercury* to a fever of excitement. "The fate of the Confederacy," it thundered, "hangs by the ensign halliards of Fort Sumter." As if in answer, as if the flag itself were fighting and refused to come down, it slipped only part way when its pole was hit, and became entangled in its ropes so that it could neither be raised nor lowered. "God Almighty," Anderson is reported to have said, "nailed that flag to the mast, and I could not have lowered it if I had wished." The pole was hit eight times before at last it fell, carrying its colors down into the flames of the burning fort. But loving hands snatched it up, and fixed it on its broken staff to sandbags along the parapet. Starvation drove Anderson to terms—evacuation of the fort with his colors flying. After the four years of struggle were ended, Major Anderson with his own hands ran that same flag up at Sumter, on the exact anniversary of his evacuation. When he died, those colors went with his casket to a grave in West Point cemetery.

The most famous flag story of the Civil War, known to all the world through Whittier's "Barbara Frietchie," is not a true incident, though it is based on the defiant flaunting of the red, white, and blue by Mary A. Quantrill, a young woman of Barbara's town of Frederick, Maryland. A year later Confederate troops were again marching northward, this time through Chambersburg, Pennsylvania, when a group of girls with the Stars and Stripes pinned on their bosoms confronted a Texas outfit tauntingly. "Ma'am," drawled one of the soldiers to the leader, "we rebels never see that flag flying over breastworks without charging them."

One good laugh all around is better than reviving a word of the old animosities, and soon after that tragic war the flag itself was an ambassador of fellowship. It is told that Gilbert H. Bates, Sergeant of the First Wisconsin Heavy Artillery, made a bet that he could carry the Stars and Stripes across embittered Dixie. His "taker" assured him he would "have his heart cut out in the first town." Bates started in at Vicksburg, a city which had suffered as much as any in the Confederacy. Newspapers had taken up his story, with the result that when he stepped off the river boat he found the bank lined with thousands of ex-Rebels— and was presented with a beautiful Union flag made by the ladies of the city. He carried that flag afoot in a nine-month tour that was a triumphal progress. Perhaps a million Southerners cheered his standard. Not one offered injury or insult.

The flag completed circumnavigation of the world for

the first time in 1790, when Captains Robert Gray and John Kendrick carried it at their masthead around the Horn and Good Hope. The same Captain Gray in 1792 sailed it over the bar of the Columbia River and so laid our claim to Oregon and Washington. With his own hands, Meriwether Lewis bore it, August 11, 1805, through wilderness over the Lemhi pass, at the headwaters of the Missouri, to raise it a few months later at Fort Clatsop, near the Pacific's shore. When the Dark Continent was crossed for the first time, our country's flag accompanied explorer Henry Morton Stanley. The American banner taken in 1902 by Mr. and Mrs. William Workman, of Worcester, Massachusetts, went to the top of Nun Kun, a peak of the Himalayas 23,394 feet above sea level. In 1909 Commander Robert E. Peary, of the U. S. Navy, with one Negro companion and a few Eskimos, raised our flag over the North Pole.

There is now a large body of traditions gathered together in "the Code of the Flag." Some outstanding points: Display the flag only from sunrise to sunset; raise it briskly; lower it slowly; do not expose it to bad weather; fly no flag above it; never loop or festoon it (use red, white, and blue bunting for that). Never cover a speaker's desk with it, but hang it behind him; in hanging the flag without a pole, keep the blue field uppermost, to the observer's left (the flag's own right). When unveiling a statue covered with a flag do not pull the flag down but lift it up and away; on Memorial Day half-mast the flag only till noon. On a casket the blue union should be at the head, over the left shoulder of the honored dead; it must not be lowered into the grave. In church the flag should be at the congregation's right.

The flag is not dipped in salute to any living person no matter how exalted his rank, or to any edifice or object no matter how sacred. Never drape the flag across any vehicle or display it on a float, except flying free on a staff. Do not sew or paint the flag on clothing, furniture, and the like; never use it in advertising. And when it is worn or faded do not throw it away, but burn it.

Many imaginative explanations are given for the "meaning" of the colors. The red has been asserted to stand for the Army, for the blood of patriots; the white has been claimed to represent the Navy and, according to the Boy Scout *Handbook*, purity. The blue has been thought to signify, variously, justice, loyalty, freedom, faith in God. But only Congress, surely, should have the power to pronounce on this matter. And it has never said a word. Nor need it. The American people know what the red, white, and blue mean to them, and are not as literal as some who try to teach them their ABC's. Nor is it true that each star stands for an individual state. In 1818, when Congress decided to keep the stripes at thirteen but add new stars as new states were born, it debated the idea of having each star symbolize a particular state and definitely rejected the idea. So all the stars together stand for all the states together— our Union, one and indivisible.

By 1912 the number of stars had increased to forty-eight. Perhaps no one thought then that any further changes need ever be made in the flag, so President Taft, by Executive Order, regulated for all civil service flags the proportions of the emblem as a whole and of each detail in its design. But now, if Hawaii and Alaska are admitted to statehood, we shall have fifty stars to accommodate. If we put in ten rows of five stars each, that will make an entirely different shape of blue field, whichever way you turn it, destroying the perfect symmetry. Far better would be five horizontal rows of six stars alternating with four rows of five stars. This would keep almost the same proportion of the blue canton to the whole. How the flag of the future will look is up to Congress, however.

But what our flag looks like when the world sees it coming is up to all of us. Americans at home and abroad can disgrace our bright banner, or they can make millions cheer and weep for joy to behold it in their skies. For its unique destiny is that it must always go forward. Our flag which has been to the Pole, and the roof of the world, and swept the seven seas, is the banner not of conquerors but of a people adventurous in brotherhood. It is the flag of a free people; its folds are lifted only on the wind of their will. And its staff, like that on Suribachi, can be implanted on new heights only by the combined devoted strength of all our hands.

Old Glory Takes to Sea

‍

*You know me and trees, Mark. You say I look for a tree
back of every bit of early American history. But am I not
right? In an age when you could hardly turn around in this
country without touching a tree, all Indian treaties, all
land surveys, all building of homes or masting of ships
inevitably brought trees into the story. Famous still are
certain "witness trees" accepted in courts of law as less
likely to lie than the human tongue, when it came to a
survey of land. There's also a long legal history connected
with the "marriage trees" of Maryland's Eastern Shore,
goal of eloping couples from Virginia. And I've seen, still
standing, the "whipping trees" and a "slave girl tree" that
have outlived the customs by which they got their names.*

*And of the three tall pines that are the heroes of my
next pages there's definite hint in well authenticated records. So, careful historian though you are, you'll let me
have my way with them, I think. . . .*

51

THIS is the story, the true story, of three trees in American history. They were white pines, and for two hundred and fifty years the white pine in our national life was king of timber trees. But these were kings of kings. Even rooted in the forest they had a look of destiny about them. For they stood three in a line, and the middle one the tallest, like the masts of some ship plowing through the green sea of boughs below them.

The center one was one hundred and forty feet tall and four feet thick at breast height, and the others were just under that. You shall hear presently how it is that we know the figures so exactly. They rose so loftily above birch and spruce that on a day too still for even the aspens to twinkle a blade, there was trouble running through their topmost branches. But those were days when all men could feel trouble coming, even in the forest depths.

Trees such as those are not grown in a year, neither in the span of man's days, nor in a century. These trees had begun to live before the Pilgrims landed, before Columbus saw the palms of San Salvador in the dawn light of an October day. Each was a great column, from deep taproot to straight crown, giving off branches in tier above tier, like the platforms of a pagoda. The branches of a white pine are lifted at their tips as a dancer lifts her fingers.

Their needles, five in a bundle, are long and slender, pliant and glossy, deep blue-green delicately frosted on the underside. When the wind stirs in them their voice is a high soft seething, unlike the harsher tones of other pines with coarser needles. So when the three foredestined pines lifted their boughs on a river of wind, like prophetic hands, they let them fall again with a long sea-sound of *hush* and *hush*, as if they were listening for things to come.

What was to come was a long time coming—as long as it took the pines to grow. It began on the other side of the Atlantic, where long ago the forests were swept away from western Europe, and where great pressures and wants were building up. There was bread hunger and land hunger, there was a want of wood, and a want of liberty, political and religious. Nothing was plentiful enough save human beings, and they were too many. Something there must break, burst free, overflow; something must find a new way, in a new world.

So the ships come sailing, tacking and veering in the teeth of the west wind, falling in the chasms of the Atlantic, rising on its white crests, till they raise the landfall of the New England coast, where the forests come swinging their boughs down to the very shore, till their needles are burned with the salt spray. Now a new people step ashore, a plain people but determined; they start inland, with ax and Bible, with gun and woman, to make this land their land. They are few at first; they are poor, but in the great virgin stands of white pine that spread north to Canada, south to Georgia, and west no man knew how far, they struck gold. Indeed, only thirty years after the Puritans landed, they were exporting white pine timber to England, to Portugal, to the Canaries. The trade ran, presently, to the West Indies, all around the Cape of Good Hope to Madagascar, and to the slave coast of Africa. For not in tropical jungles, indeed not in all the world, was there mast wood like this, or happier wood for millwork. White pine built the towns and villages, the churches and mansions of New England. It built Beacon Hill doorways, and the grave fanlights under Portsmouth elms. It roofed the families and filled the pockets of the Americans who claimed it as their right.

Never was there a wood so smooth and straight of grain, so easy to work with the plane, soft even among the softwoods, yet strong in proportion to its weight. Some of it cut like cake, under the drawknife and chisel. It was satin-smooth, gleaming white, unresisting, buoyant. And the famous carvers of the days of the clipper ships loved it as a man his bride. From it they cut those figureheads that sailed the seven seas. Years after the clippers were gone, the old figureheads—American eagles, American goddesses—lay staring still into the sun, amid the corals and the pirates of Sunda and Barbary.

It is all gone now, that virgin timber wealth. You may blame our ancestors for their prodigal ax work, but pine was their first resource; they spent it the way today we spend our income. It was theirs because they had earned it, by hardship and daring, the pioneer's way. And it seemed to them that this resource was inexhaustible. The trees grew so thick you couldn't turn a sled around at the end of a lumber road without cutting enough timber to make a thousand sleds. You couldn't "fall" a tree without

knocking down two. You couldn't "roll" or "snag" three
of them down to the river, without cutting down a hundred.
Back in England a tree had meant an ancient elm or oak by
the dooryard, a fountain of shade at your window in summer, in winter bare of leaves and letting in the light. Trees
there were family friends. Here they were of a density
like a matrix, and the white pine was the gold in the ore.
A man called a "landlooker" would climb some lofty,
easily mounted spruce and sight under a shading hand for
"veins of pine," as they called them, that flowed like a dark
river through the paler green of oak and walnut. Then he
would fling down a branch to point the direction of the
far-off groves, and so the way to them could be found by
compass.

Through the woods the shipwright would then come
riding. He would look every likely tree up and down, as
the sergeant looks at a recruit, guessing his height and
weight at a glance, knowing what sort of heart is in him.
The shipwright would know just where every kind would
go in a ship—elm for the keel, and yellow birch for the
keelsons, beech for the garboard strakes, and a straight
trunk of oak for the stern post. In every crotch he saw what
he called compass timbers; simple angles of trunk and
bough for the catheads, and great forks for the wing-tran-
som knees.

But pines, of course, were his passion. Gray pine he
viewed with contempt—crooked and good for nothing, he
called it; pitch pine was no use save for the tar in it for
calking seams; red pine was too heavy and short for his
business, though it made good deals for the deck and was

strong in the beam. But white pine he sought out, as a gem merchant seeks to match precious stones, because it is so free of knots, so straight, and buoyant, and resilient in a gale—the lightest and least top-heavy stick that ever went into a mast. Gigantic sticks, these that grew in American woods, and all of a piece. Never had the shipwrights of Britain, who had for centuries been piecing together stubs of resin-heavy Riga fir, seen such masts as those that were coming to them from New England. So from the time of William and Mary, when the first forest laws for America were passed in distant London, the white pine was a marked pine. Marked by the King's Broad Arrow— three slashes with an ax on the trunk.

This was the blaze of tyranny, as the hot American woodsman saw it. This was the edict, as it went forth from the faraway throne of fat King George:

> "All pine trees fit for masts, of the growth of twenty-four inches diameter and upwards of twelve inches from the earth shall be reserved to Us, our Heirs and Successors, for the masting Our Royal Navy, and no such trees shall be cut on penalty of the forfeiture of such grants, and all other Pains and Penalties as are or shall be enjoined and inflicted by any act or acts of Parliament passed in the Kingdom of Great Britain."

Such pains and penalties included fines and imprisonment for those who cut the King's pines, and flogging for those who disguised themselves as Indians to do it. Serious cases were tried by courts of Admiralty—as if a man who cut a tree with the King's Broad Arrow on it were a pirate!

It made the colonists boil to have risked their scalps combing redskins out of the woods, to have let the first sweet sunlight fall on the ground they had won, only to discover that years before some hireling of the King's had been here branding the flesh of good New Hampshire trees.

The servants of the Deputy Inspector of His Majesty's Woods in America would drive loggers from their homes, seize their timber, and burn their mills, all according to Forest Law. But the colonists went by what they called "swamp law," and where it ran the King's sawyers found the Broad Arrow mockingly marked up on trees so rotten at the heart they fell apart as a mass of toadstools when lifted out of the mast pools at Portsmouth. The sound and fit pines had often been sawn up into small lengths, and quietly floated out of the colony to Connecticut.

So it seems plain that destiny itself, as I claim, guarded my three tall pines both from the free American ax and the King's dooming blaze of the Broad Arrow. For still they lifted untouched their boughs to the rising wind of trouble, as though to welcome it. That wind was running now through the American people, as the first blast of winter went sweeping through our forest, flinging the red of maple leaves into the seaward rushing rivers of New England, stripping the white oaks bare on the Dutch farms of New York, whipping up the waves on the Potomac where it swings past the broad acres of a gentleman farmer named Washington, and dying away at last in a sigh through the bearded moss upon Georgia live oaks. So, variously, the colonies were troubled, with the Stamp Act, and the Forest Laws, and the Townshend Acts, and all other acts of Parliament passed without consent of the governed.

There were pacific men on both sides who sought adjustments, proposed compromises; there was Doctor Benjamin Franklin over in London, printer, postmaster, and inventor, who spoke very ably to Parliament on behalf of the colonists; and in New Hampshire there was Governor John Wentworth, a popular, forbearing and cultivated gentleman who tried to get the back-country folk to see the sweet reasonableness of the King's way. Each man met with a deal of success—and it did no good whatsoever. You can catch wind in a bag, and pull the drawstring tight, but that does not stop the wind from blowing.

And when wind first strikes a tree it troubles only the nearest leaves, but branch after branch becomes lifted by it, till there is no leaf that is not thrashing; and at last the whole trunk may thrum from root to crown, upon a deep vibration. So the peoples from the root of Georgia to the tip of Maine, who had hardly known each other, who— the king thought—could be separately punished or rewarded or seduced, shook together in one vibration of anger.

But always, in such times of high purpose and struggle, there are fat cats to fish in the troubled waters. Such a one must have been the Tory merchant who secured those three tall pines to mast a ship he was building, a West Indiaman. His lace-wristed hand had signed their death warrant, and doubtless taken snuff thereafter. So in the great cool forest the axes sounded, laid to the moss-grown roots. The deathbed was prepared, of smaller trees felled to lie pliant and take up the shock. At last there came a cry of rending wood—sound wood to the core, limber and straight and all of a piece—the shouts of running men, and a long sigh as the crown swept in an arc through the sky, a sigh that said, "So be it." Three times did a king die like that, with a great expiration. Then the chains strained, and the twenty yoked oxen strained, and men's shoulder muscles strained fiercely, as one by one the three great timbers were worked through the forest over the log road built for them, to the stream that would float them to the Piscataqua, and down to the yards on Badger's Island, at Portsmouth.

The West Indiaman was intended for the Guinea trade. The ship was to be laden with good white pine till the water line reached toward the gunwales. The stout pomaded owner, himself sitting snug in his mansion, would send it then staggering under all sail over the Tropic, to the slave coast. There the supercargoes sold white pine for two-legged ebony. Then they ran this wailing, reeking cargo on the Trades to the West Indies, sold it into chains, loaded up with Santo Domingo mahogany—(fine furniture that made, for the Portsmouth mansions)—and, adding some sugar to sweeten the whole business, raised a sheet for home, last leg of their three-cornered run. So the trade had been shaping for years, and the Tory merchant had grown fat on it. But there were lean men in New Hampshire shaping a different future.

You wouldn't know, to walk the quiet streets of Portsmouth today, dappled with the shade of ancient elms on fine porticoes designed by Bullfinch and McIntire, that a city so aristocratic could ever have been arch-rebellious. When, on December 14, 1774, the mob and militia took the Castle, Governor Wentworth sent out a call for every loyal New Hampshire man to rally to the defense of his King. There came to his aid four members of his privy council, two aged justices, one sheriff armed with a billy stick, his own private secretary armed with a quill, and his brother-in-law who, being eighteen years old and armed with nothing, must be accounted brave.

From the capital to the villages, that same spirit ran. John Stark shut the water gates of his sawmill, kissed his Molly good-by, and started gathering a regiment, man by man, as he galloped down the road, till he roused all New Hampshire and sent it tramping through the June grass to the top of Bunker Hill.

Bunker Hill, Trenton, Princeton, and then came Bennington, in August of 1777. There had been a thunderstorm in the night, but the day, bright and hot, was fine for a battle. You've heard how General John Stark said, "There, my boys, are your enemies, the Redcoats and Tories. You must beat them, or Molly Stark sleeps a widow tonight." In the hottest of hand-to-hand fighting the New Hampshire boys saved her from that.

Meanwhile, in Philadelphia, Congress that summer penned two Resolutions, passed in the same hour, and so wrote the history of my three pines.

"Resolved, That the Flag of the Thirteen United States of America be Thirteen Stripes, Alternate Red and White; that THE UNION be Thirteen Stars in a Blue Field: Representing a NEW Constellation.

"Resolved, that CAPTAIN JOHN PAUL JONES be appointed to Command the Ship RANGER."

As Jones himself liked to put it, "That flag and I are twins, born the same hour from the same womb of destiny. We cannot be parted in life or in death. So long as we can float, we shall float together. If we must sink, we shall go down as one!"

So Captain Jones came to Portsmouth to superintend the building of the *Ranger*. That's history. Portsmouth even remembers some of the girls at the quilting party who worked with scraps from their best silk gowns on the new flag for the handsome hero. Mary Langdon, Caroline Chandler, Augusta Peirce, and Dorothy Hall set their stitches with fiery pride, and proudest of all was Helen Seavey, married that May, as she cut from the skirts of her bridal gown the thirteen shining stars.

While in the parlor the needles flashed, in the shipyard the hammers cracked and the saws went shining. This was to be a ship that "could run like a hound"—"the sauciest craft afloat." So boasts Portsmouth's Elijah Hall, who went aboard as second lieutenant. He it is who records the fact that the giant masts in the sloop *Ranger* had been intended for a 400-ton Indiaman. How Jones got hold of them, whether their Tory owner fled, or sold out like his kind, is lost to us in the wreathing mists of those battle-smoky times. We are plainly told, however, that those three heroic white pines were too lofty to suit Mr. William Hackett, the celebrated shipbuilder who designed the *Ranger*. Even when they were trimmed ship-size, she'd be "over-hatted," he said, shaking a disapproving head.

"She'll always sail uneasy and crank, and you'll be in peril if she has to claw, close-hauled, to windward in a squall. If you'd cut those sticks down to something reasonable, I'd feel safer for you."

John Paul Jones laughed in his face, and looked with love at the great shafts soaring skyward above them. Not an inch more would he let them cut off. "Give me a fast ship," said he, "for I intend to go in harm's way."

Harm was piling up—for the British. Bennington was followed by Bemis' Heights, and Freeman's Farm, till, beaten on the right flank and the left, unable to advance on New York or retreat to Canada, Burgoyne surrendered at Saratoga. A messenger started right from the battlefield, and rode without stopping for thirty hours and some two hundred miles, to Portsmouth, where the *Ranger* lay, ready now to sail. Into the hands of Captain Jones was delivered this pregnant news, which must go with all speed to Dr. Benjamin Franklin, our ambassador to France. Ultimate victory itself might well depend on its swift delivery.

"I'll have it there in thirty days!" boasted Jones. And on the first of November, the *Ranger* cleared Portsmouth for the sea, every rag of canvas crowded on and straining. From her mainmast fluttered a banner, a new flag in the skies of the world.

North and east on the Great Circle swept the *Ranger*, through snow and sleet and winter gales, and never a stitch of sail would her captain take in, though she came close to beam-ends. But the great masts held; under their load of canvas they sang with a deep thrumming, and fought back at the gale. The life of the men aboard that ship, the crucial news that would bring France into the war on our side, were all dependent on the soundness of that wood. Three hundred and eight tons of oak and pine, cannon and shot, were driven now by a winter gale through the ancient resistance of the sea. White pine, New Hampshire pine, trees grown clean and strong in the air of freedom, brought that burden into port. Brought John Paul Jones to Franklin's rooms in Paris, brought recognition by the French court, and money and arms, men and ships, to Washington's aid. Gun after gun, ship after ship, saluted the *Ranger*, and the new flag she flew, as she sailed through the French fleet at Quiberon Bay; cheer after cheer wafted over the waters. That was the first salute our flag ever received from a foreign power. And over the rolling smoke of that ceremonial gunfire rose tall and straight—three in a line and the middle one the tallest—the great white pines that had grown, after all, for this hour.

The American Eagle

Symbols, so eloquent to the initiate, are untranslatable.

I have here, spread upon my desk, the photographs you sent me of the Cambodian coronation parade, and your letter about it. "It started in the early morning, since the brutally hot sun here would make a long midday procession impossible. Alice and I watched it from the street. As I am so much taller than the average Cambodian, I had no trouble in viewing the whole thing, and I put Alice up on top of a wooden box. It was quite something—elephants, brass bands, and finally the King and Queen, borne on a royal palanquin. The King traditionally is supposed to stop at three different places on the parade route to change vestments, but since he is fairly old and has been ill, he refused to do more than change his hat.

"For the whole of Coronation week the Royal Palace was open to the public every night, and we wandered through the throngs taking in the fantastic beauty of it all. And on the last night we were invited to attend the Royal

Dances at the Palace. The great pavilion was filled with all the glitter and pomp of a big European opera house, but with an Oriental splendor. In the center was a vast carpet for the dancers; on the far wall stretched a huge mural of the giant stone faces at Angkor Wat. To the right the King and Queen had their seats, on either side of them the chiefs of mission of the entire diplomatic corps, in evening dress and medals. Opposite were all the lesser members of the corps, and members of the Cambodian government and armed forces in full dress. (The Cambodian formal dress is a curious mixture of East and West; above the waist is a stiff white jacket with a close-fitting high collar; below this is worn a one-piece skirt-like affair called a sampot, the longest part of which is drawn up between the legs and tucked in behind, giving a sort of knickered effect.)

"The dances themselves were accompanied by a variety of strange Oriental instruments—zither-like things, drums, and gongs—and by a group of women who told the stories of the various dances in a high wailing chant. Each movement carried an intricate meaning, and one of the most exquisite effects is the way in which they can bend their fingers back almost to their wrists, as they are trained to do from early infancy . . ."

And much more just as colorful, together with one picture after another of these smiling monarchs glittering on their ornate thrones. But what I linger over is a view of the procession showing great floats of creatures (mounted on jeeps) which, you explain briefly, are Garuda birds. And I know that you and Alice travel sometimes through those Eastern lands on the Garuda Airline. What, I ask myself, *is a Garuda? Since my ornithologies fail me, I am sent to the dictionary. There I learn that the Garuda is "a super-natural being, half man, half bird, with golden body and red wings." Very impressive. We have nothing half so gaudy. But I'll give you now a bird that stands as a symbol from one long coast of ours to the other, and I'll match him and his meaning with any other in the whole wide world.*

🐦

THE United States of America has a king. He shows himself in every state in the Union and in the territory of Alaska, and is seldom seen outside this country except in the dominion of our friendly neighbor, Canada. He is a king of the air, the undisputed ruler of high American sky, the American or white-headed eagle.

As a proud monarch should, he has regal features—a snowy head, an aquiline nose, a piercing eye. In fact, he bears a distinct resemblance to Uncle Sam himself. The eagle was officially placed on the Great Seal of the United States by act of Congress on June 20, 1782, while Uncle Sam, as an impersonation with familiar features, only began to show his face in newspaper cartoons more than thirty years later. So it's true in this case too that people grow to look like their pets!

Congress chose well when it picked this species for the national emblem, rejecting the golden eagle which was originally proposed by the designer of the seal. This darker bird, also found in the United States—though rarely west of the Rockies—for centuries has been a heraldic symbol in such undemocratic states as Czarist Russia, the Austrian Empire, Napoleonic France, the Prussian Empire, the Roman Empire, and indeed of tyrannies and dictatorships running back to Assyria. Handsome it may be; cruel it certainly is; as a harrier of young stock it has a thousand marks against it for every one that can be charged to the American eagle, whose favorite diet is fish. Honest old Ben Franklin, who wanted to make the strutting and stupid turkey gobbler our national bird, charged the American eagle with being a coward, a bully, and a verminous thief. He did not know, apparently, that this bird of our choice is more attached to its home, is more faithful to its mate, and spends more care in the education of its young than any other in the skies.

Eagles mate for life. This is claimed for many birds, but usually falsely. The eagle pair do stick to each other, in breeding season and out, until death does them part. Only then will the bereaved one disappear for a while from its accustomed haunts to roam the skies—now so often empty of eagles—till somewhere it finds a new mate and leads it home. Courtship begins earlier in the year (or later, if you prefer to call November that) than that of any other of our birds. And it lasts longer, continuing until June. In their eyrie, usually at the top of a very tall tree not far from water, the couple live in fierce and ardent devotion. There seems reason to think that the mating act is repeated, at dawn and sunset every day, until the eggs are laid and even after—as if the union were not for reproduction only. One ornithologist tells of the wild cry that rings out from the mating birds, over the tops of the trees steeped in shadow and awed silence.

No other bird is so deeply attached to his home. The eagle never leaves his bailiwick, except to seek a mate; he does not migrate. Most birds desert their nests at the end of one season; it is to them not a home but a cradle. The few that, like cliff swallows, return to the same nest, do not enlarge it. But the eagle each year builds a new nest on top of the old one. And an eagle may live as long as a man—longer, up to one hundred and twenty-five years. So the nest grows and grows in grandeur, and serves not only as a cradle but as a permanent home for the parents, summer and winter. One nest in a tree that blew down near Lake Erie was found to weigh nearly two tons, and represented perhaps a century of occupancy. Another, found on a rock off the California coast, contained twelve wagonloads of sticks and leaves. Coarse branches sometimes six feet long formed the breastworks of this bird castle. Within, it was lined with soft grasses, lichens, Spanish moss, and feathers. And the view from such a wilderness mansion is usually the grandest in the countryside.

The female eagle lays two or three white eggs. The

egg of a hummingbird is bigger! That is, in proportion
to the bird that lays it. Not three inches long, an eagle egg
is smaller than the Canada honker's and only half the size
of a whistling swan's. From such small beginnings grows
the king of the air.

Both parents take turns at incubating, which lasts for
about thirty-five days. Without stirring, one bird will sit
as long as seventy-two patient hours. When very weary it
will signal the mate with a chittering sound. Then the
change of guard will be made swiftly and quietly. If an
eagle must absolutely leave the nest unguarded, the saga-
cious creature will rough over the top of the nest with
dead leaves to make it look deserted.

The eaglets, being born so small, have a long infancy.
And the life they are going to lead is so much more complex than that of most birds that their education is long.
At first the chicks get food popped into their mouths, but
when they should begin to feed themselves, the parents
tear up a fish before the youngsters' eyes to show them
how to do it. Presently they bring a whole fish and stand
back while the little fellows learn to quarter it themselves.

Eaglets in their nursery play with sticks, just as children
play with toys, and learn to grasp objects with their talons.
Before they can fly, they must first pluck out the gray down
they were born with, and then preen their new, strong
flight plumage. They are taught to exercise every day. Their
parents show them how to jump up and down, on the
ample platform of the eyrie, flapping their wings. They do
this by the hour, squealing and stamping the while, like
children in a game. All this is preparatory to flying, and to

fly as an eagle flies is something that, it seems, is learned only by weeks of practice.

At last the young eagles make a first terrified fluttter from the edge of the nest. Usually they tumble back in again as fast as they can, scared but apparently proud and excited. If they are too slow about trying again, the parents discipline them by withholding food. Shriek with hunger as they may, the youngsters are not fed, but tantalizing morsels are dangled back and forth just beyond their grasp. When at last an eaglet completes his first solo flight, he gets a reward of food.

Like girls and boys approaching maturity, young eagles, once they can fly, spend less and less time around home, until toward the end of their first year they go off to seek their own fortunes in the world. They do not mate until in the fourth or fifth season they begin to wear the snowy crest and white tail of the adult, but long before that they are on their own as masters of all they survey. Their tremendous wingspread of seven or even eight feet is matched by an internal strength of their great pinions. The longest primary feathers are twenty inches long, the quills an inch in diameter where they enter the skin. The wing tips are slotted; that is, the eagle can spread the primary feathers apart like fingers. This is a feature of all birds which can soar, glide, and even rise without flapping the wings. It seems to act as an anti-stalling device, much like the slotted wing of the airplane invented by Handley Page. He found that a slotted wing increased the maximum lifting power by 250 per cent at an angle of 42 degrees. Ages before, the eagle knew how to bend his wing upward and forward at the tip, with the result that the air is deflected over the wing top, leaving the main shank of the wing free to function several degrees beyond the stalling angle.

With such an equipment, the eagle is the absolute master of flight. He has been found, by airmen, flying at 9,750 feet above the earth. With his marvelous eyes he has been known to detect a fish three miles from the spot where he was soaring and capture it in one long slanting dive. It is this power that makes him the dread of the fish hawk or osprey, whom the king of the air frequently forces to drop his fish, the eagle recovering it as it falls, with marvelous dexterity.

His fishing skill has also earned him the hatred of fishermen who will not share their luck. In Alaska, where reckless commercial exploitation of the salmon runs brought the canning industry to an all-time low, a bounty of fifty cents was put as the price on the head of the national bird. Stringent laws regulating the take brought the industry back till it produced eight million cases a year. But the bounty, on the twenty thousand breeding pairs of eagles officially estimated to remain in all the Territory, was raised to a dollar. Later, fortunately, the bounty was wholly abolished.

The eagle has many dangerous enemies—all of them human. Since Congress gave it the kiss of death in 1782 by publicizing it as the national bird without giving it legal protection, the eagle has had to fly through a barrage of lead and raise its young in the midst of its ill-wishers. For a century eagle eggs were at a premium with the class of collectors who rightly called themselves "fanciers." And unnumbered thousands of dusty, molting, stuffed eagles still adorn the top shelves of drugstores, barbershops, and country offices. Every farmer who misses a hen thinks, if there is an eagle nest about, that he may pay it a punitive visit. Added to injury is libel—a charge so criminal that, if it were true, it would justify the vicious attacks on every eagle pair. But there is no truth in the hoary newspaper story of the eagle who snatches the baby from its cradle. No American eagle has ever been known to make an unprovoked attack upon any human child. For twenty-five years the National Audubon Society has patiently followed up each one of these accusations, and in every case it melts away to fable.

Only in the last few years did Congress get around to passing legislation to protect the symbol of our proud freedom. Except in Alaska, it is now unlawful to kill, or shoot at, or capture Uncle Sam's birds, or to take eagle eggs or molest the nest. The enforcement of this law is no stronger than the vigilance of game wardens and the attitude of country judges.

So, if ever you find an eagle's nest, run right home and tell—nobody. News of it will spread from your best friends to the eagle's worst enemies. Every hunter who thinks he must kill whatever fair and shining mark dares stir, every curiosity-seeking robber, will learn of it. So, when you come again, there may be no eagle. Then you can take a silver dollar out of your pocket, or a quarter if you're feeling cheap, and apologize to the brave emblem. But the American sky over your home will be lower than it was.

In spite of all that Americans have done to exterminate

their grandest bird, it is still not uncommon wherever the fishing is good. It is most abundant in Alaska and Florida, around the Great Lakes, along the Mississippi River system, and off the coasts of the two oceans. Wherever you saw it, you never forget your first American eagle. He may be sitting in motionless unblinking majesty upon the highest limb of the tallest tree in all the countryside, keeping guard over mate and nest, over wood and water. Or you may first have seen him taking a power dive from the skies, uttering his war cry as he stoops to pounce upon the shapes that stir beneath the waters. Or perhaps you have watched, as I have, a flock of eagles soaring, circling, rising up around one another until they become specks against the blue. Then it is not the dark spread of wings that vanishes last, but the flash of the proud crest, like the twinkle of snow on distant mountains.

Father Serra's Rosary

It's a fine thing to hear the eagle scream and to wave our national banner. I'm proud of a son who carries that over the sea, but it's clear to me, as I read over these letters from Southeast Asia, that a Cultural Affairs Officer of the USIA is a missionary of an admirably liberal sort. For he makes no attempt to destroy beliefs and customs in order to replace them with his own. Rather he offers some of the gifts of his own way of life freely, to no disparagement of those alien to and more ancient than ours. The young, of course, are nimblest at accepting these offerings, and we in the United States are used to welcoming students from foreign lands— though it is, I confess, curious to hear of the President of the Cambodian Ping-pong Federation coming to study sports and physical education with us, and a Prince of the royal blood who will learn about police administration at one of our major universities. Come to think of it, the strangeness is no more than must be felt by the Olympic swimmers you received in your hot tropical town, from

*various American colleges, to show their prowess to the
interested Khmers. Or by our famous decathlon champion
who "went over with a bang, and drew a crowd of ten
thousand in the stadium, plus hundreds of Cambodian
functionaries."*

*You send us teachers, too, as well as students, from that
Buddhist land. "The Venerable Brah Boddhivamsa Vajir-
appano Huot Tath is going, clad in his saffron robe and
sandals, to lecture at the Harvard Divinity School and other
academic and religious institutions. Arranging his program
was more than complicated, owing to the religious restrictions involved. First of all, he couldn't travel alone, not
only because his religion would not permit, but because he
does not speak a word of English and only a smattering of
French. We're sending an interpreter along with him who
will act as his disciple. Then, he cannot eat solid food between the noon of one day and the dawn of the next. This
involves cables to Pan American and his hosts in the U.S.
He may handle no money, nor ever sit next to a woman, let
alone shake hands with her. For this special seating arrange-
ments had to be made on the planes. If possible, he re-
quested, he would like to spend his evenings in a pagoda.
More cables to Washington: what have you got over there
in the way of Buddhist pagodas? (He courteously agreed to
hotels where necessary.)*

*"But all in all it is very much worth the trouble. The
Venerable is a charming and frail old scholar, friendly but
reticent, other-worldly but warm. I'm sure some of the
pleasantest memories I will ever have will be of the quiet
chats I had with him, arranging his visit, in his peaceful,*

palm-shaded temple. What he will make of America—the roar and bustle—I don't know. I hope they keep him bundled up in that Boston winter, and give him enough rest."

And suddenly I think of another robed religious teacher who came into the American wilderness almost two centuries ago. He was a frail scholar too, yet time has not erased his footprint from the land. Just now, as I write, there floats out over my garden the deep-throated chiming of bells from one of the missions of which he dreamed— the only one whose altar light, from the long-ago day of its kindling, has never been extinguished.

WHILE George Washington was still a loyal subject of King George, and Dan Boone was oiling his rifle for his first trip into Kentucky, another pioneer, nearly three thousand miles farther west, was exploring the remotest corner of the future United States. Father Junípero Serra in his gray Franciscan robes was no less daring and resourceful, no less visionary of the future greatness of a new land, than the English-speaking pioneers. And he was just as much an American as the *Mayflower* settlers. For, like them, he had been born in the Old World

and had come a painful way to build in the New a better
home; at the age of fifty-five Serra had cast in his lot for
life with the fate of the wild, wide North American continent.

It was on July 16, 1769, that Father Serra first said Mass
at the foot of a cross overlooking the fine harbor that is
today San Diego's. There and then he dedicated the first
of the twenty-one famous missions of California. "Father
Serra's rosary" they are affectionately called. But the little
band of men—fellow Franciscans, a few soldiers and some
Indians from Lower California—were witnessing more than
the beginnings of the great "mission system." They were
present at the actual founding of California itself, neglected
as inaccessible for two hundred years.

Better perhaps than even the military commander of the
expedition, Gaspar de Portolá, Serra foresaw the vast con-
sequences of the new venture. He dared to dream, there in
that arid, sun-scorched wilderness, amid hostile Indians,
with men dying of scurvy, of a land glowing with the
orange, and rippling with grain, inhabited by peaceful
Christian people.

Father Serra, born in 1713 on the island of Majorca, was
not the type one would pick for a pioneer. A scholar, a
doctor of theology and professor of philosophy, he was a
frail man who suffered from chronic bronchitis. He had
received an injury to one leg that made walking an agony,
yet with sandaled feet he was to trudge six thousand miles
on his apostolic labors. He hardened himself to sleep on the
ground and live on roots and seeds. While the soldiers and
Indians were fighting and killing each other, Serra passed

unharmed among "the gentiles," his "pagan children" as
he called them.

Not primarily for the saving of pagan souls had the
government of King Carlos III of Spain sent Portolá to
explore and defend Alta (Upper) California, but to fore-
stall the Russian Bear which was reaching a paw down the
Pacific Coast from Alaska toward California. However, the
Crown recognized the value of the Franciscan missionaries
in pacifying the Indians; and it planned in its own time
to secularize the converted red men and transfer them to
civil administration. But to honest Father Serra all this new
land was the Indians'. Even the mission buildings were to
be theirs, and all the cattle and sheep, all the farms and
produce of the mission system were to be held in trust by
the Franciscans, who themselves owned nothing of this
world's goods.

Within a year Serra had founded another mission almost
400 miles farther into the wilderness, on the shores of
Monterey Bay—the Mission of San Carlos Borromeo,
known as Carmel Mission. The next year, in an oak-studded
valley of the Santa Lucia mountains, blazing with July
heats, the dauntless Serra slung his bell from a gnarled old
tree and tolled it to the unresponding silence. "Come, gentiles, come to the Holy Church; come and receive the faith
of Jesus Christ!" he cried.

Not a pagan was in sight. Yet the cry of the bell had
spread through the forest. Presently an Indian appeared
and looked on with awe as Serra said Mass under the cross
he raised. Given presents, the Indian returned with others
of his tribe. All grew to love Serra, and he set about learn-

ing their language. Together the men in gray robes and the men in their bronze nakedness raised the first crude structure that was the Mission San Antonio de Padua.

For the mission "churches" of these first, brave, struggling years were not the solid and shapely structures we see now with their six-foot walls, their carven doors and painted ceiling beams, their gardens and fountains, their bells and cool cloisters. Such structures blesséd old Serra dreamed of but seldom saw completed. The first "missions" he knew were but rude shelters of boughs and bulrushes. Yet the missions of today stand pretty much where Serra and his successors first planted the cross. Not whimsically were their sites selected. Serra, realizing that he was fixing the seat of future settlements, searched for abundant water, good soil and climate, timber, and a location on the coastwise highway of which he dreamed. And on the sites he selected grew up San Diego, Los Angeles, Monterey, and San Francisco. Of the nine missions Serra started, only San Antonio today has no town around it.

When Serra had founded four missions and been in California three years, troubles that had been brewing came to a crisis. The new country had not yielded quick returns either in revenue or converts; the colonies had cost more than was bargained for. Every item of equipment and almost all food still had to be brought an immense distance by small sailing vessels. The Indians, indignant at the treatment given their women by the soldiers, retaliated with arrows and firebrands. San Diego mission was burned, its padre killed. All the others were in danger.

Both the Viceroy of New Spain (Mexico) and the Father Superior of the Franciscans back in Mexico City were in-

clined to retreat. So Serra set out for the capital—a round
trip of 2400 miles—to save the California venture. For
talking points he had no material gains, and few spiritual.
He had only his shining vision and the conviction of absolute truth his words seemed to carry.

And he got all he asked for: the right to found more
missions; more money; an overland road to California; and
the immigration of more settlers, especially of families and
of women to provide wives for the soldiers. Instead of
retreating, the Viceroy and the Father Superior were persuaded to pour in fresh blood and treasure. Serra returned
to found Dolores (San Francisco), beautiful San Juan
Capistrano in the hills near San Diego, San Luis Obispo
and San Buenaventura on the Santa Barbara channel coast.

In the seventieth year of his age, having confirmed more
than five thousand heathen converts, noble old Padre
Serra felt his last reserves of strength ebbing. On foot he
made the round of his nine missions, from San Diego to
San Francisco. At each he bade a sorrowful farewell to his
brother Franciscans and the weeping Indians. Death found
him at Carmel Mission in 1784. The double tolling of its
bells brought the grief-stricken Indians, who came with
wildflowers to lay upon the redwood coffin of the Apostle
of California.

Serra's successor was Father Fermin Francisco Lasuén,
who founded nine missions, including Santa Barbara,
Purísima, Soledad (Solitude) near Carmel, San José near
San Francisco bay, San Juan Bautista near Carmel, San
Miguel in central California, and San Fernando in the val-
ley of that name.

Only three missions were added after Lasuén ceased work:

Santa Iñés near Santa Barbara, San Rafael across the bay from San Francisco, and Solano in what is now the "wine country" of the sunny inner coast ranges. To the surprise of all, the Russians sent gifts and good wishes to the founding of these last two, the padres' "farthest north."

Father Lasuén, an even greater administrator than Serra, brought the mission system to its highest peak of influence, efficiency, and prosperity. It was his ambition to make the missions self-sufficient. At them the Indians learned more than fifty trades, so that a mission could employ carpenters, stonecutters, shoemakers, wheelwrights, cowboys, and sheepherders. The Indian women were taught to spin, weave, and make clothes. Tallow, hides, pottery, baskets, blankets, saddles, soap, candles, and wine were produced. The missions grew many vegetables; oranges and lemons were planted, and olives, almonds, walnuts, figs, dates, fruit trees, and grapes. Great fields of wheat, barley, corn, and oats were plowed and planted. Between 1783 and 1832 the twenty-one missions produced 4,137,625 bushels of food for the Indians and struggling colonies; and they may have had as many as 150,000 head of cattle and perhaps as many sheep.

Irrigation works were started by the Franciscans. They dammed streams, built reservoirs and aqueducts. Beautiful fountains adorned many of the gardens. The water also turned grain and olive mills. Some of these hydraulic systems are still partly in use by the towns and ranches of California.

The chain of missions, spaced approximately a day's ride apart, became the inns of the voyagers of those days. Clean, quiet, cool, secure from Indian hostility, they must have looked like heaven to the weary folk who came to their doors. And there the traveler could converse with men of breeding and education, or read in the mission libraries.

The location of the missions largely determined the route of the Camino Real, or King's Highway, first worn smooth by the toiling Franciscans, later broadened to accommodate the trains of *carretas*, or wagons, from Mexico. When the United States entered on the conquest of California, it found the footsteps of Serra almost the only line of military communication. Today U. S. Highway 101 and the coast route of the Southern Pacific railway follow approximately the old Camino Real.

In Father Lasuén's day almost all the mission churches began to take on much the appearance that the best pre-served of them have now. Without being trained architects, the Franciscans had to solve their own structural and artistic problems. From bitter experience they learned that nothing is so likely to fall down in an earthquake as a wall of stone blocks or of adobe. So walls as much as six feet thick, often supported by buttresses, give the missions their air of strength. Frequent fires proved that thatched roofs were impractical, and so the Fathers showed the Indians how to make tiles, and now that colorful and harmonious type of roofing is characteristic.

The bell tower, or at least a bell frame, was a prominent feature of the missions. The padres were addicted to the sound and use of bells, while the Indians venerated and delighted in them, too, for the language of bells can be understood by all. So bells have come to be the very symbol of the California missions. And time has only mellowed their tone. Even to a Protestant like myself, the tolling of the mission bells, to which I wake each morning, chimes its way into the rhythm of living.

Within the mission churches the native art of the Indian was given sway. Most of the original mission doors are deeply carved with parallel waving lines—the Indian's symbolic "river of life." The wise Franciscans permitted Indian artists to make their own form of offering to God.

So friar and neophyte worked out together a distinctive style in architecture and decoration. With their softly flowing lines and delicately tinted surfaces, the missions are deeply harmonious with their natural setting. They look kind— tranquil, hospitable and strong. They have served as the inspiration and model for a whole California style; and if not all of this is equally good, that is no fault of the originals.

Just when the missions had reached the height of their usefulness and beauty, and had become the one civilizing force holding the frontier communities together, a deadly blow was directed at them, first by the Government of Spain and later by independent Mexico. The missions were secularized—reduced to parish churches with a single priest, and stripped of everything except the buildings themselves. Many of the pioneering padres, men of education and high ideals, were supplanted by inferior friars, some none too intelligent or holy. Then the lands which the Fathers held in trust for the Indians and had brought to high productivity were given in immense feudal tracts to settlers from Mexico, the *rancheros*. The Indians, who had given up their native life for the white man's way, were stripped of both at once, and so driven to beggary or to acts of violence. As the missions fell into despair and were abandoned, the governor,

Pío Pico, sold them off at auction, enriching himself with commissions.

By the time the American armies came, in 1847, the missions were in a sad state, some serving as stables and liquor cellars and for other profane uses. Only Mission Santa Barbara was never abandoned and never passed out of the control of the Franciscans. True, only two of their number were left; still they remained in the neglected shell of the once great church and cloisters, guarding the precious records of the whole mission movement.

By 1888 the people of southern California had become so conscious of the heritage of beauty in the missions, and so indignant at their neglect, that they formed the Association for the Preservation of the Missions, under the leadership of Charles F. Lummis, the writer and historian. Largely to save the northern missions, the California Landmarks League was organized at San Francisco in 1902, and soon the societies of the "Native Sons" and "Native Daughters" joined in a state-wide campaign to pick up the scattered pearls of Father Serra's rosary.

Walls again were raised, and roofless altars covered again from rain and dust. Profane objects were swept away, both within the missions and, where possible, in the immediate suroundings. Sacred objects, once mission property, were rediscovered where they had fallen into private hands and many of them were bought or donated and restored to their place. Protestants of the community joined in; some who could not give money gave their labor. At Santa Iñés a band of wandering hobos saw the struggles of restoration and worked for weeks to help.

Some of the missions which had not actually suffered neglect or outright theft had suffered from excessive attention. Local congregations and parish priests had sometimes tried to disguise the mission origins; wooden steeples had been added; walls had been breached to admit sickly stained glass; beautiful old Indian murals had been smeared over with whitewash; just about every conceivable atrocity was committed with the best of intentions. It was a task to get this undone, and it is not all put to rights yet.

San Rafael Mission had totally disappeared; Soledad is a hopeless adobe rubble, fast melting away; Sonoma is turned into a local museum full of Civil War and pioneer relics. But millions of tourists from every state make the rounds of those that are left, following a path marked out for them by the State of California, with mission bells as signs. Each mission has its beauties and charms, but certain ones—Santa Barbara, Carmel, and San Juan Bautista, for example—have long been special favorites because they are so nearly what they were in their great days, both in completeness of original structure and as "going concerns" today, with the Franciscans again or still in charge, with fine libraries and gardens, and spacious and interesting settings. Others that are off the main-traveled roads have an especial lure, such as Santa Inés and lonely San Antonio where so long ago Serra slung his bell and tolled it.

I see, every day in the year, a crowd of people around the "river-of-life" doors of Santa Barbara Mission. Whatever their denomination, Americans cannot but find new faith for the fight for Christian democracy in such serene survivals of a pioneering godliness.

Washington—Your Capital

The capitals of the world make a kingly roster. Paris, London, Berlin, we say, and see again the noble avenues, the ministries, the monuments all made familiar to us by their comprehended history. Moscow and Warsaw, Peking and Budapest ring in our ears like iron. But of the capital of Cambodia I confess I knew nothing, until there came to my hand this one of the many magazines published in many tongues by USIA, *Free World*, which is circulated in nine languages to thirteen countries in the Far East.

"Phnom Penh," it tells me, "at first sight is a jangling, banner-hung, modern Asian city under a blazing hot Cambodian sun. There is the sound of gongs and cymbals from morning to night, a constant stream of gaily decorated bicycles and once in a while festive parades. In the teeming city of Phnom Penh in addition to Cambodians there are Malays, Chinese, Annamese, a few Indians and Europeans.

"As Cambodia is a Buddhist nation, the saffron robes of priests are everywhere and the suburbs are dotted with aging pagodas and hallowed bonze graveyards . . . It is also the meeting place of four waterways, so the city naturally became a commercial center and today ranks second to Saigon as an outlet for the 'Golden Peninsula' of Indo-China, exporting rice, fish, cotton, rubber and forest products. Along the river fronts are weathered boats waiting for cargoes . . ."

And down those streets I see you go, with Alice, distant as figures seen in a Lorraine glass. Yet even there you are guided by the pulse of another capital, our own. Via the cable and the diplomatic pouch, Washington is closer to you than I am here on the Pacific Coast. It is headquarters; you know it as a soldier knows his base. But the fun of showing it to you first was mine; we took each of you brothers East to see it the year he turned fifteen. A lot of American fathers believe in this rite of initiation. For you it marked the beginning of a long dedication. . . .

Evɛʀʏ year two million Americans (or more than twice the resident population of the District of Columbia) pour into our national capital. We the people take it like some right guaranteed in the Constitution that we should one day make a pilgrimage to Washington's altars of history. So happy crowds climb thousands of monument steps, tramp echoing miles down corridors of state, visit every famous sight from the cherry blossoms foaming around the Tidal Basin to the outlined footsteps of John Wilkes Booth on his dread course through Ford's Theater.

Yet Washington is more than a collection of sights. It is a symbol of our national life, the story in stone of the best of our ideals. The long slanting thoroughfares fatefully named, like battleships, for the states, the succession of monuments, the great buildings speaking through their architectural styles of the march of our history, are more than reminders of our past. They are timeless in meaning; so they speak to us also of the future. There is an air of destiny about this place, of great things yet to come. Here you feel the pulse of the living nation. And here, no matter what state or territory you come from, you can feel at home. For only Washington is every American's city, your town and my town, ours to take pride in, ours to show our children for the good of their citizenship, ours to grumble at, from Congress to climate.

Foreigners are surprised that our governmental center is not located in our largest city. But imagine the Washington Monument wedged between the Chrysler and Empire State buildings, or the Unknown Soldier shaken in his tomb every thirty seconds by the subway! Uncle Sam would be a sadly jostled old gentleman were he overwhelmed by the wealth and busyness, the decibels and skyscrapers of Gotham. Indeed, before Washington was founded, New York was tried as a capital, and then Philadelphia. As a result of these experiences, the wise fathers of our country decided to free the councils of state from the pressure of banking and mercantile interests and local politics, by establishing a District of Columbia as sanctuary for the federal government.

Congress, having selected the banks of the Potomac as halfway between North and South, appointed our first president to choose the best spot. A country squire, he loved the woods and templed hills, broad meadows and streams, spaciousness and gracious views. So Washington, D. C. began as an ideal—in the mind of Washington, George. Then it acquired buildings and, last, a population. That is the reverse of most cities' evolution, but it is putting first things first.

What Washington needed, to build the federal city which was later to bear his name, was a man with a plan, a great plan for a great country's capital. He also needed a landscape architect, surveyor, engineer, and artist, though there were no funds to pay so many experts. In Major

Pierre Charles L'Enfant, Washington discovered them all combined in one man. Trained military engineer, L'Enfant had come over with Lafayette, at his own expense, to fight for American independence. Drillmaster for our raw troops, artist-extraordinary to the army (he painted Washington at Valley Forge), L'Enfant was a deep student of city planning, and burning with ideas of his own for our capital. To Washington and Jefferson he unfolded these schemes.

First, with their co-operation, he picked the most commanding sites for future public buildings. These he proposed to connect by broad avenues. Throughout the city he projected squares and circles to contain monuments and statues to heroes yet unborn, and from these, radial thoroughfares intended to give long vistas. So to the French engineer our capital owes its enduring symmetry and direct communication between points, and its beauty full of surprises. The visitor never knows when he will suddenly have a glimpse of some stately dome, some heroic figure, some leaping fountain. A glance at the map shows how living L'Enfant made his city. It looks like the structural diagram of an organism, balanced in its parts, nourished by vein and artery, heart and pulses.

Jefferson, that ardent amateur architect, had been all for a rectilinear street plan—straight streets meeting at right angles to form square blocks. But on such a plan public buildings can be seen clearly only when you are directly in front of them, and too close under them to grasp their true form. More, traffic between any two points in a rectilinear city is always along two sides of a triangle. In the end, Jefferson's ideal and L'Enfant's were combined,

and what we have is a wheel-and-spoke pattern laid down
on a checkerboard system. The slanting thoroughfares of
Washington cut off miles and hours of travel, and pour
her traffic along the shortest possible lines.

With full confidence in the architect, Washington en-
thusiastically recommended him to the Congress. But when
it got wind of these ambitious schemes, it foresaw what
seemed extravagant expenses, splendors deemed unsuited
to a young, struggling nation. The Capitol building, as
designed by Latrobe the architect and Thomas Jefferson,
was considered far too large—and it was but one third the
size of the present building. The whole office force of government then comprised only one hundred and twenty-six
persons, and here was L'Enfant laying out a city intended
to accommodate a population equal to that of Paris! Plainly
he was a dreamer, and a dangerous one. Congress found a
good pretext to drop him, and with relief saw him depart,
into poverty and obscurity, with his plans under his arm.

Already the city had been sketchily laid out, the sites
chosen for the principal public buildings; the White House
was under way and the Capitol begun—tradition says
George Washington turned the first spadeful of earth for
it, and stood under a great elm to watch its progress. By
1800 the capital was officially occupied; the Adamses moved
into the "President's House," the legislature met in the
Senate wing (the only completed part) of the Capitol,
and the creaking wheels of the raw young federal government began to turn.

But the vision of a noble federal city was dimmed by the
greed of speculators. By agreement with the original land-

owners when the site was chosen, every other lot was granted to Uncle Sam, the sale of which was to defray the cost of his public buildings. For the sites of these he had paid twenty-five pounds an acre. The acreage for his streets had been granted him. But the lots remaining to the original owners were theirs to sell without restrictions. And now, L'Enfant's plan neglected, the desecration began. Many landowners chopped down all their trees, to crowd in more dwellings; parts of the city looked like a cut-over lumber tract. Pennsylvania Avenue, the chief artery between White House and Capitol, grew up as a jumble running into cheap hotels and shops. The Mall, intended as the fair open heart of the city, became its open sewer. A railroad was later permitted to thrust its tracks and throw its smoke right across the center of the town. The District of Columbia, voteless, voiceless, kept as though on charity by federal appropriations, became known as the stepchild of Congress.

But from the first, and ever since, there have been patriots, in Congress and White House, and outside, to see beyond the city's swamps and dumps and slums to the vision of what had been intended and might yet be. One who had this exactly in mind was Andrew Ellicott, a surveyor who had worked in L'Enfant's office. Able to remember every detail of the Major's vanished plans, he was wise enough to scale them down to something Congress could contemplate without a sharp pain in the budget. And Thomas Jefferson started early to repair the deforestation by planting the first of those rows of street trees that today make Washington the leafiest great city in the country. So, good men and greedy working together and against each other, the city rose. When the Civil War came, the Washington Monument was completed only one third of the way, and the Capitol dome was unroofed and looked like a gigantic open pot; it would never be finished, said those who believed the Union could not survive. The necessities of war swelled the city's population and dotted it with temporary war offices, barracks, hospitals, prisons. When these were removed in Grant's administration, the city was a pockmarked, misused, deflated organism.

Then there appeared on the sleepy Board of Public Works an ex-plumber, a master fixer, one Alexander Shepherd. Enormously vital, politically powerful, backed by the courageous newspaper publisher Charles Noyes, Shepherd proceeded to wake up the Board, Congress, and the landlords with a start. He tore down old nuisances that had long been condemned; in one night, he demolished the rat-infested city market; in its place rises now the public library. When a railroad refused to abandon its grade crossings and defiantly ran an engine out across a street, Shepherd ripped up the tracks, leaving the engine looking silly. Foreseeing the city's growth, he began paving streets and planting trees in cow pastures—which are now considered close in town. Unable to substantiate a claim of dishonesty against Shepherd, Congress dismissed him for exceeding, by millions of dollars, the legal debt of the District. It took fifty years to amortize the debt; no one has ever succeeded in undoing all the good that Shepherd did our nation's capital.

But every experience of trying to protect the basic plan

and augment the beauties of Washington had come to grief through Congress which, after all, did, and should have, the final word. To succeed completely, the movement must start inside the Capitol. Senator James McMillan of Michigan it was who, in 1901, began the long uphill battle. To aid him, McMillan called in the services of such great men as Augustus St. Gaudens, the sculptor, the architect Charles McKim, Frederick Law Olmstead Jr., the distinguished landscape architect, and Daniel Burnham, leading spirit in the Chicago World's Fair of 1892. These busy men dropped their lucrative careers to devote most of their remaining years to a master-plan for the nation's capital. At last, after almost all the devoted leaders were dead, their plan, like the cherry blossoms in April, burst into flower in the nineteen twenties and thirties. "Temporary" structures that had stood since World War I were cleared away; magnificent buildings rose on Constitution Avenue, parks were linked with parks and graced with monuments.

So today the United States of America has a capital worthy of it. To see the master-plan of the city in a glance, you have only to ride to the top of the Washington Monument. There you can see that the axis of the whole system is a chain of parks in the form of a long cross. At the intersection stands the Monument. At the foot of the cross, to the east, rises the Capitol on its hill. The park that links Capitol and Monument is the Mall, lined on both sides with splendid public buildings. Looking to the west, you see at the head of the cross the Lincoln Memorial, exactly in line with the Capitol dome and the Washington Monument, and separated from that by the Reflecting Pool, a long mirror of water in which the image of the Monument is caught. Out on the arms of the cross are, to the north, the White House amid its trees and lawns, and to the south the Jefferson Memorial, its dome rising softly above the cherry trees.

Built in the classic style Jefferson loved, the doors of the Memorial stand as open as his mind. On the four walls, you read his thoughts. "We hold these truths to be self-evident," begin the deathless sentences on one wall. Another quotes from his great statute on freedom of worship, a third his prophecy of the abolition of slavery, a fourth his warning that laws and constitutions must be changed to fit the progress of the human mind. And around the circle under the self-supporting dome, in letters two feet high, is graven: "I have sworn upon the altar of God eternal hostility to every form of tyranny over the mind of man." The heroic-size bronze likeness shows Jefferson at the age—only thirty-three—when he wrote the *Declaration.* Of all statues in the capital it seems most nearly alive. The lips might just have spoken the words that ring like great music from the walls. The eyes gaze lovingly toward the Virginia hills where he was born. He who so loved invention, can almost hear, one would say, the friendly roar of the planes forever circling the skies of Washington.

The Jefferson and the Lincoln Memorials are more than monuments; they are temples. And in each there is an oracle. As we stand in them, looking and listening, these oracles speak to us, not with supernatural tones nor in riddles, but in voices that we know and love, in phrases that we have by heart. So on the walls of the Lincoln Memorial are inscribed in full the Gettysburg Address, and the Second Inaugural Speech, and every moment of every daylight hour, throngs of people are reading those words in slow reverence. Then they go again to look up at the sorrowful wisdom of the giant sculptured Lincoln in his chair and, renewed in their American faith, descend the long flights of gleaming stairs. Looking back at the great oblong temple, you can see that every detail of it has meaning. The thirty-six Doric columns—one for each state in Lincoln's day—which encircle the building, are triumphantly surmounted by the names of the sister states, reunited after their quarrel that broke the great heart and took his life.

As for the Washington Monument, it is not only the tallest memorial ever raised to a man, but one wholly perfect. It is perfect in fulfilling the Greek ideal of beauty, which is strength combined with grace. It is perfect in its proportions which reveal the secret of the Egyptian obelisks, the height, five hundred and fifty feet, being just ten times the base of fifty-five feet square. And it is perfectly appropriate. In its soaring integrity, it is a "speaking likeness" of the hero it commemorates. It speaks of a man, foursquare, upright, and lofty in ideals, who swerved as little in adversity as would the Monument itself. Sir Cecil Springfield-Rice, British ambassador in World War I, called it "George Washington's finger pointing to the sky." Visible from most of the important rooms in the White House, it has been the inspiration of harassed Presidents since it was completed in 1884. One could wish that everybody in the federal government daily measured himself and his work by that great standard in stone.

Riding back over the river into the city, you feel that the flags everywhere ripple more bravely. Every day in Washington is Flag Day, for each government building must fly the Stars and Stripes. So, looking out over the capital's roof tops, on a fair day, you see, rising out of the sea of treetops, hundreds of flags near and far. To these must be added the banners of the stately embassies; these foreign colors proclaim what daily becomes plainer to the world—that Washington is not only the nation's capital, but the strong heart of freedom to whose beat all the world is listening.

City of tossing flags, city of old trees, of flashing fountains and fine bridges, city of science and research, of scholarship and art treasures, Washington has a grandeur serene above national politics. Indeed, the visitor to Washington, if he is wise, leaves all his political notions behind him. He can afford to do so, for it is by his will, and yours and mine, that the Ins got in and will be thrown out again, that the Outs will get in again before we put them out again. Whigs and Federalists, Democrats and Republicans —through the years they have all been no more than the guests of the American people, in the most beautiful city we know how to build.

The White House

🌾

"The Royal Palace" (so I read on in Free World) "has
many separate buildings in Khmer style, the most famous
being the Silver Pagoda, floored with five thousand blocks
of solid silver. The Pagoda houses royal family treasures, a
collection of Buddha images fashioned of gold, jade or
other precious materials, and gifts which the family has
received. Palace attendants, in the ancient Khmer way,
wear a different color sampot each day, and only the King
has a six-tier umbrella."

I don't know how to match that, I admit. Our President
wears nothing grander than a Homburg hat, even on the
day of his inauguration. As for his home, the floors are
mostly only wood. But it's a nice place; as folks say, "We
like it."

E VERY four years the American people go to the polls to decide who shall live in the White House. Far younger than Vatican, Kremlin, or Buckingham Palace, the home of the Presidents is as precious to the American people as are those splendid piles to Catholics, Russians, and British subjects. More modest than any palace, smaller than many a rich man's residence, the old white mansion at 1600 Pennsylvania Avenue, set back amid lawns and shade trees, is what the citizens of this land like to think of as the best they have to offer to the best man they can find to live in it.

The pride we feel in the White House goes far beyond the ownership implied by the few cents that a taxpayer gives to its upkeep. It has been from our country's beginning the seat not only of executive power but of an ideal of American family life. A national shrine, it is still a home which has known such joys and sorrows, births, marriages, and deaths as yours and mine. Through history, we have shared in these; we are proud of the fourteen brides who have been married from this gracious home, of the two silver weddings celebrated there, by the Hayes and the Tafts, and of the twenty babies born in the upstairs rooms. Steeped in good traditions, dyed with rich history, the President's home enhances the dignity of his office, and this can only operate more powerfully with each succeeding administration.

From the day that a coat of white paint was laid over the gray Virginia sandstone of which it is built, the people of the nation have called it the White House. The elegant Federalists of the early Republic preferred "the Presidential Palace"; for half a century it was officially called "the Executive Mansion." But it kept on being "the White House" to the public, and when Theodore Roosevelt came to office he had its official name changed, by authorization of Congress, to what the people called it. It's typical, of the house and of the country, that the popular name in the end won out. It was the people too, during the Truman administration when the grand old mansion was found to be unsafe because of decay, who demanded that it be restored just as it then stood. Far cheaper would have been an entirely new building, but Americans insisted that their first home of the land be reconstructed as they knew and loved it.

The original plan for the White House was drawn up by Captain James Hoban, Irishman by birth, resident of Charleston. He won a prize of $500 offered by Congress for the best design. Time has proved that it was a noble one, conceived on lines of simple classicism and adapted in spirit to the use intended for it, though it has been necessary to add wings, as inconspicuous as possible for the business of the Executive Department. Fifteen decades of whimsical fashion have passed through the interior, affecting furniture and draperies. But the house itself, though the oldest public building in Washington, has never gone out of style.

On October 13, 1792, just three hundred years after

Columbus discovered America, the cornerstone was laid. It's unsettled whether George Washington wielded the trowel that day, but he certainly didn't live to occupy the building. Labor troubles, Congressional slowness, and national poverty combined to delay the work so that it was still not finished, and less than half furnished, when the Adamses threw open its doors at the first reception, in 1800.

Only fourteen years later this fine new First House of the nation was burned by the British, in the War of 1812, while spirited Dolly Madison reigned there. It isn't true that Mrs. Madison saved the Constitution, or the Declaration of Independence, for they had already been rescued. But she did delay, while the British were advancing with torches but a few blocks off, to have the great Stuart portrait of Washington unscrewed from the wall of the State Dining Room and carried to safety, while she herself took charge of the White House silver.

Fortunately Major Hoban was still alive to guide the reconstruction after the war. The walls were undamaged, and by the time that the fashionable Monroes entered it, a finer White House opened its doors once more. From then on, it has gone through much the same evolution as every other old American home. At first it was lit by simple candlelight, till in Fillmore's day, in 1851, gas came in— an admired marvel, then something merely useful, and at last, toward the close of the century, a detestable old device to be got rid of for the new sparkle of electricity which illuminated the administration of Benjamin Harrison. From stables on the White House grounds the President's coach—or in winter his sleigh—came prancing to the door, till William Howard Taft squeezed himself into the first gas buggy. It was Mrs. Taft who instituted the custom of twin beds, and removed the great Lincoln bedstead to the guest chamber.

For it is the privilege of each new First Lady to banish outmoded styles and rearrange the house that is now her home. It is her duty, too, to remove all broken and worn gear—and the wear and tear in this center of national hospitality has always been terrific. So the house has been a mirror of American taste. For instance, the East Room, the grand reception hall where once Mrs. John Adams was obliged to hang out her wash to dry, passed from a stately Colonial style through the ornate decoration of Lincoln's time, and became pompous, in Cleveland's era, with dark soggy colors, circular sofas, potted palms, and tortured moldings. Then Theodore Roosevelt banished the carpets for a bare inlaid floor, replaced the fancy chandeliers with cascades of crystal, and so made it the show room and the truest to period of the mansion. From Teddy's time on, the White House has been conscientiously restored, especially by the Hoovers, to the best periods in American decoration, the Colonial and early Federal.

Even the eighteen acres of grounds have come far from the days when Jefferson had a snake-rail fence around them and Mrs. Lincoln kept a cow on the front lawn. Many a tree set out as a sapling by a President now gives deep shade. Of course, in a city grown to a million souls, the neighbors can no longer be freely admitted, save when their children come on Easter Monday to roll their eggs on the lawn. That custom started when Washington kids were chivied from

Capitol Hill, and President Hayes invited them in. Garfield defended them when authorities tried to exclude them. Wilson put them out; Harding welcomed them in again.

There have almost always been children in the White House, to make it ring with their cheers or tears. The country likes to have them there, and follows their doings delightedly. Tyler used to play forfeits with them in the Red Room. Jackson never tired of giving parties to the friends of his seven grandchildren. Willie Lincoln drove his pet goats right through the front door; Theodore Roosevelt's youngsters roller-skated in the halls and tried riding bicycles down the Grand Staircase. The White House, that has seen so much of pomp and some of sorrow will, we hope, always reflect happy young faces too.

Visitors to the White House have, from its first opening, been a constant stream, of the great of earth and the humble, from Lafayette to Cherokee chiefs in war paint, from the King and Queen of England to Will Rogers. Formal receptions are held in the great white and gold East Room. By day it is half darkened and one tiptoes in some awe across the bare parquet under the eyes of the famous Stuart portrait of Washington. In the three enormous crystal drop chandeliers slumber by day prismatic rainbows, waiting to shine again, when the lights are lit, upon the glittering orders of diplomats, and the jewels of ladies. Here have been held the time-honored New Year's receptions, at which any citizen might come to shake the President's hand. Here in the Civil War, when the rain or snow roused old Abe's pity for troops camping in the streets, soldiers bivouacked, invited in by the President, with all their wounds and mud and vermin.

And in this room have lain in state the bodies of Presidents William Henry Harrison, Harding, and Zachary Taylor, who sickened and died in office, of Lincoln, Garfield, and McKinley, martyrs of assassination, and of Franklin Delano Roosevelt. At such times, the whole room has been draped in black, even the chandeliers swathed in it, lest one sparkling dart of light should awake there and recall the joys of weddings and dances and children's parties.

Next to the East Room comes the Green Room, an informal place for the welcome of guests, then the Blue Room, which is a little gem. Oval in shape, in graceful Colonial style, it is a fit setting for small formal receptions. Here the new ambassadors are received on their first call upon the President, and members of the Supreme Court, of Congress, and high officers of the armed forces. Beyond lies the Red Room, where you will wait until your hostess arrives to take you to luncheon in the smaller dining room. The State Dining Room, scene of historic feasts, is paneled in English oak, cheered by an immense stone fireplace and lighted by a silver chandelier. Gone are the big game heads with which Theodore Roosevelt proudly animated the walls: Mr. Harding sent the trophies to a museum, and Mr. Hoover brought the Healy portrait of Lincoln down from the attic to hang there.

The rooms upstairs do not belong to the public now, but in earlier days the presidential family knew but little privacy. Dickens found the long wide corridor crowded with men on state business, messengers, petitioners, curious sight-seers, and lobbyists. Next to his study on this floor, Lincoln had a telegraph office which chattered the news of the battlefields. In the hall, they say, Lincoln walked at night when he could not sleep, up and down, up and down.

Lincoln's study was carefully restored by Mr. Hoover with the furnishings that the Great Emancipator knew. In this room, his biographers believe, Lincoln signed the Emancipation Proclamation and there hundreds of Congressional bills, and half a dozen Amendments to the Constitution have been signed by his successors. Next to the study comes the Cabinet Room, where in many a time of national crisis the course for the ship of state has been tensely plotted.

Beyond lies the President's Library, oval in shape like the Blue Room beneath. There are six bedrooms on the second floor; most of them, at some time, have been occupied by the President. But few care to sleep now in the cavernous, dark Lincoln bed. It was in this bed that Lincoln had a dream, two weeks before his death. He had been up very late waiting for dispatches from the front, and had no sooner fallen asleep than he dreamed he heard loud sobbing. He thought he arose and went downstairs. All the familiar rooms were lighted, yet all were empty, the Red Room, the Blue Room, and the Green Room.

"I kept on," he told his wife and a friend, "until I arrived at the East Room. Before me was a catafalque on which rested a corpse wrapped in funeral vestments. Around it were stationed soldiers; there was a throng of people, some gazing mournfully upon the corpse whose face was covered, others weeping pitifully. 'Who is dead in the White House?' I demanded of one of the soldiers. 'The President,' was his answer; 'he was killed by an assassin!' Then came a loud burst of grief from the crowd, which awoke me from my dream. I slept no more that night."

I asked Mrs. Roosevelt, as we stood in the upstairs corridor, if the White House is haunted. "In the daytime one never thinks of such things," she smiled. "But sometimes, late at night, when you step out in the hall and everyone is sleeping, you feel the presences of the other lives."

And the American people feel the presence in the White House of those lives, so many of them faithful and strong, some few immortally great. In a crisis we cluster at the gates or stare by night at the lighted windows. On the night of Sunday, December 7, 1941, when the news of Pearl Harbor had broken, about a thousand people spontaneously came together around the White House. Through these gates hastened generals, admirals, cabinet members, diplomats, newsmen. The crowd outside, shaken by the torpedo that had struck the ship of state, could not enter, could not know what grave decisions were taken within. But somehow it comforted these watchers just to draw close to the home that embodies the spirit of all American homes. And however we vote in election years, we all say *Amen* to the prayer written for that house by its first occupant, John Adams:

"Heaven bestow the best of blessings on this house, and on all that shall hereafter inhabit it. May none but honest and wise men ever rule under this roof."

The Capitol—Home of Congress

❧

"Storm clouds," you write, "are lowering outside the window, a great gust of cool wind is rising, and in a few minutes we shall have a drenching tropical rain. I was up on the roof of our building a few minutes ago and watched the great black clouds scudding along over the city and on down the Mekong. From the roof you can see the tops of the Royal Palace peeping over the trees, and up the main street one can make out the great gray finger of the Phnom sitting squat on its hill in the center of town. The Phnom is the temple-crowned hill after which the city was named. Hundreds of years ago a princess, Penh, saw a vision here of Buddha, who pointed downwards signifying that this would be a prosperous place to build. This is the last of the Cambodian cities, Angkor having preceded it by centuries. When we wander here, Alice and I, we find it hot and peaceful up on the top of the hill, with a few dark brown

Cambodian boys, who follow us, smiling and curious. . . ."

I can send back no photograph as strange as this you send of the temple topping the hill of your ancient princess. But our capital city also has a focus of its genius loci, and "The Hill" is what they call it. There serenity has no place at all. Peace in the Capitol, I suppose, would mean that we were all as dead as Angkor Wat. And yet the wrangling and obstructive talk instead of thought up there has made me break out in wrath so frequently that it's a family joke. "There's Father stamping his cane at Congress again!" I hear you chuckle across the continents and seas. I know, I know. All of us need a whipping boy for our despairs. And the Congress of the United States, thank God, is tough enough to take my puny tempers. Those men have to be, to wrestle with the living sinew of this democratic system.

Some of these men I know and love, like Douglas of Illinois. Some I detest; they shall be nameless here; in short historic time they will be forgotten if not forgiven for their sins. But all of them, I think, would be the better for going up on the roof (to speak in a figure) to look out far beyond the borders of their constituencies, of their country even, to see how wide and various a world it is, and where the storm clouds lower.

But storms and tempers die, argument wears thin at last. Something remains, under the dome, that makes the place a shrine to the most vital political force on earth. So for your Phnom, I give you back the Capitol.

PROUD upon an eminence, with its wings widespread and its lifted white dome thrust to the fore, our Capitol, like the American eagle itself, looks out over Washington. The city was still only a dream in the head of Major Pierre Charles L'Enfant when in 1791 he rode with George Washington up Jenkins Hill, to point out to the first President how this rise of ground was a very "pedestal waiting for a monument." That monument to our democracy came thus to stand at the hub of L'Enfant's wheel-shaped plan for the city—and indeed, of the free world's politics today.

For this grand old building is a focus of global attention. From its broad steps, where Lincoln spoke of "malice toward none and charity toward all," each new President's inaugural address rings out into history. More, the resolutions of the Congress that sits here decides the destiny of some 164,000,000 Americans, and every Foreign Office on earth bends an ear to the Capitol's famed "whispering gallery." And your own voice, through your vote, finds utterance here.

From its conception, the Capitol was as dear to George Washington's heart as if it were the Constitution in stone. Tradition has it that he himself, wearing a Masonic apron, laid the cornerstone on September 18, 1793, while cannon boomed salute to the future, and a five-hundred-pound ox turned sizzling on a barbecue spit. As the walls rose, despite labor troubles, Congressional apathy, popular misgivings, the father of this newborn country wrote that "it is the progress of that building that is to inspire or depress public confidence." Today, no less, the progress within it sends high or low the spirits of the American people.

Designs for the home of Congress had been invited by a competition, in which the prize offered was the munificent sum of $500 or a medal, plus a lot in the unbuilt city! The specifications were for a building containing two lofty chambers for Senate and House, each capable of holding three hundred persons (spectators included), with two lobbies and twelve offices, for committees and clerks. The Founding Fathers never dreamed that such an edifice would not suffice for the business of the United States Legislature, as far as they could peer into the future.

The judges of the competition—Washington and Jefferson—were inclining toward the plans of a Paris-trained architect, Stephen Hallet, when they were offered drawings by Dr. William Thornton of Philadelphia, physician, wit, painter, poet, and horse breeder, who was then but a novice at architecture. But this first product of the genius he later developed for it established the core of the building we know today, and won him the prize. The disappointed Hallet was put in charge of the construction, and promptly substituted many of his own schemes for those of the winner. He was discovered and dismissed, but only after these ideas had begun to take shape, so that this house of our two-party system was from the beginning formed by successful compromise.

And it reached completion only by virtue of endless amendments. Congress, like any home builder today, was galled by unforeseen costs, sometimes into ill-considered economies such as replacing skilled architects by army engineers, chief clerks, or even the postmaster of the city. And rascally contractors cheated Uncle Sam; the shingle roof leaked, wall plaster crumbled, a chandelier fell out of the ceiling, an arch under the Senate chamber collapsed, killing one of the architects. Worst of all, from a Congressional point of view, the acoustics were so faulty that precious pearls of oratory floated to the roof and were lost.

Yet by 1812 the Capitol was, for all its defects, complete in the modest dignity which befitted that era. Rich decorations, fine portraits of our early statesmen and Revolutionary heroes adorned its walls; it housed a wealth of precious documents, as well as the Congressional library, already a notable collection of books. Then war with Great Britain broke upon the nation. In August of 1814, by a surprise dash up the Patuxent River, the British fleet under Admiral Cockburn landed forces which captured the defenseless capital city. President Madison fled with his cabinet. Cockburn gave orders to destroy all public buildings. Only the Patent Office was saved when the redoubtable Dr. Thornton threw himself before the cannon set to begin its demolition and shamed the enemy into sparing it. But in the Capitol Cockburn mockingly took the Speaker's chair of the House of Representatives and asked for a vote on whether to "burn this harbor of Yankee democracy." The ringing "Ayes" had it. When the noble building resisted attempts to ignite it, the soldiery tore out books, papers, and portraits, piled them in a heap in the center of the hall, poured tar on them, and set the pyre aflame with rockets. Even the enemy was shocked; several British officers recorded their horror at the scene, and London newspapers denounced Cockburn's barbarism.

The gutted walls alone remained intact when peace brought the opportunity for reconstruction. Its director was a distinguished expert, Benjamin Henry Latrobe, whose talents had been noted by President Jefferson, himself no mean architect. To Latrobe are owed many lovely details in the crypt, notably the use, atop the columns, of purely American motifs like ears of corn, and tobacco leaves instead of the conventional Greek acanthus. His work was carried on by the gifted Boston architect, Charles Bulfinch, who contributed the great east steps, one for every day of the year. But hardly was its home rebuilt when Congress realized that the structure had been outgrown. The nation which had started out as a shoestring of thirteen little states on the Atlantic seaboard had spread, by 1851, clear across the continent, rounding out its present boundaries.

The first Congress ever called on Capitol Hill had adjourned for lack of a quorum. Now both chambers were packed, as the forces of the South, the expanding West, the abolitionist Down East were locked in tense struggle under the eyes of the visitors' galleries. Hundreds of clerks jostled each other for space. Offices must be found for members from the new states. The library was bursting out at the seams and oozing down the corridors. And the Supreme Court, at first sometimes dismissed as soon as it met because there were no cases for it to consider, was now elbowing judiciously for room in this crowded ark.

So were begun (with cornerstone oratory by Daniel Webster) the two great wings, in one of which the Senators presently established themselves, in the other the Representatives. But tragically the improved house of Congress was to be divided against itself. At the lightning flashes of the approaching Civil War, the Southern legislators prepared to depart, old friends, with ashen faces, bidding each other farewell. Hard on the heels of these seceding members, the first Union troops marched into the city. Now the Capitol was commandeered by military authority, and 1500 beds crowded the stately halls and chambers, while a bakery set up for the commissariat in the center of the building menaced the books of the Congressional library. It took an order from President Lincoln to oust the Army and let the country's lawmakers return to their half-empty halls.

The dome, at that time, stood uncompleted, open to the sky like a great caldron. Visible both south and north of the dividing Potomac it was eloquent in its arrested growth of the nation's dilemma. None saw better than Lincoln himself how vital it was that, before the eyes of all, this lofty symbol should reach fulfillment. Thus, while the wartime debt of the government grew by a million dollars each day, and the federal city itself seemed time and again about to fall into the hands of the Confederacy, nevertheless tier by tier the dome rose, topped at last by its gigantic figure of Freedom. Two hundred and eighty-five feet above the eastern plaza it soars, a miracle of engineering, with an inner dome inside of the great shell of the outer, each so constructed that its cast-iron parts can move harmlessly with expansions and contractions resulting from temperature changes. By day it shines cloud-white from afar over the leafy countryside. By night, illumined with giant floodlights, its nine million pounds of metal seem to float above the world's most powerful capital like our dreams of enduring peace.

Old-style though it is, and sometimes more grandiose than grand, the Capitol superbly meets the needs of even today's nation, since Senate and House offices, as well as the Library of Congress and the Supreme Court, have all moved out into handsome houses of their own. Esthetes may wince at the art of the historic old building, architects since its foundation have all known how to design a better, and engineers of today could certainly devise a more efficient structure than this vasty old pile. Yet with all its faults Americans love it still. One million tourists a year clamber up all its steps, mill about in the Great Rotunda, and tramp the corridors after the guides. To them, to you and me, the great white edifice on Capitol Hill is the Big Top of the two-ring Congressional circus, where we expect our lions to roar and our clowns to make us laugh.

For here you can watch in action the men you sent to Congress. You can see them, in the lobbies, considering the proposals of various interests, organizations, and just plain citizens. You can attend any committee hearing except a very few closed for reasons of national security. By calling at the office of your home-state Senator or Congressman, you can obtain a ticket to the reserved seats in the galleries to hear the debates upon the floor.

If you expect fireworks, you may be disappointed, for the discussion often seems long drawn out and leading to invisible objectives. But when a crucial issue is coming up, the air begins to tingle, the press boxes are jammed, galleries are full, messengers hasten to and fro, and down there the honorable gentlemen hammer out arguments that will travel around the world.

Yet "the Senate chamber is the Senate on display; the committee rooms are Congress at work." So I was told by one of its most distinguished members, who with his wife —herself a former Congresswoman—was generously taking me on a tour of the whole Capitol. As he spoke, we were standing in the most historic and beautiful of these committee rooms—the original Senate chamber, which was later turned over to the Supreme Court. Stately but intimate, this mellow spot reverberates with moments of past greatness. Here, said the Senator, was ratified the Louisiana Purchase; here was declared the Monroe Doctrine; here Webster, Clay, and Calhoun made their most famous speeches, and before those rich red curtains the Supreme Court handed down decisions which shape our lives today.

But the most moving moment in a Congressional session, my friend confessed, is at the opening of Congress when Senators and Representatives meet together in the House, to stand with bowed heads while the chaplain invokes the guidance of God upon their deliberations. Here, too, they hear the President's message upon the state of the union.

And here, at the tensest moments in our nation's history, the President has appeared before them to ask for a declaration of war.

In earlier days the House met in what is now Statuary Hall, which holds a collection of indifferent, bad, and excellent sculpture. Each state is allowed to place here the figures of two favorite sons (though one of the best is in the corridor outside—Jo Davidson's delightful study of Will Rogers). This was the room where Congressmen, when they used to sit here, had so much trouble with acoustics. At the spot (now marked by a brass star in the floor) where even a whisper bounces back, the desk of Congressman John Quincy Adams stood, and he once irritably interupted himself in a speech to ask "the gentleman who keeps echoing my words" to be quiet! Here, too, Adams was fatally stricken with apoplexy, dying in an adjoining room.

Threading a way through the crowds of staring visitors, the Senator led us into the Great Rotunda, while uniformed guides pointed out his own leonine head as one of the sights of the place. It is full of them—giant historical canvases, heroic-sized statues of our great, and high in the eye of the dome overhead a glowing canopy painting. In this lofty ceremonial place have lain in state the bodies of all those of our Presidents who have died in office, and of other statesmen and heroes; here too the Unknown Soldier rested briefly, while thousands of reverent fellow citizens filed past to pay him tribute.

Yet for all its monumental splendors, the Capitol provides practical and satisfactory working quarters, cool, spacious, and quiet. "As self-sustaining as an ocean liner," the Senator called it, with its own post office, machine shop, carpenter's shop, plumber's shop, even an arsenal in case of riot! He talked of the 432 rooms and fourteen acres of floor space, requiring, it is said, a small army of employees for operation, and of the page boys who go to a school of their own in the building, a school complete with cheers, yearbook, and athletic club. He told how books from the Library of Congress across the street come upon demand on a conveyor belt. He took us, too, upon the miniature subway train which carries the Senators from their offices to the Capitol and back, and to the Senate restaurant.

Here under the great chandeliers we found gathered famous faces, men who steer this ship of state upon its course. Some were heroes to me; some stood for all I most strongly oppose. Together they are Congress, of which the Capitol is only the outward frame. And together they maintain our government by just that principle of opposing thrust which upholds the great symbolic dome itself. So it is that here, through fierce partisan struggle, through windy debate and obscurity, our freedom forever flies high, like the flag itself. At forts and post offices and other Federal stations throughout the land the colors are lowered at nightfall. But from above the parapets of the Capitol, Old Glory never comes down, riding out the sunset, flying even in storm.

The Library That Thinks

A library, in the sense of a group of chosen books, is a set of windows to look out upon the world, through which, also, one can look into the mind that selected them. The shelves that are your horde, my son, garnered from boyhood on, are a pleasure to me to visit, since I see you there. And I go there often to find facts in which my own bookcases are sadly lacking.

History has the best of it among those books in your deserted study—military history, naval history, the history of our Civil and our Indian wars, a rank of handsome volumes on the British army which you acquired at Foyle's on a soldier's leave in London, and here and there a sprinkling of those small-typed and dimly illustrated memoirs by some peppery retired colonel, on his skirmishes at Khartoum or the Khyber Pass, or about ventures in a gunboat up the Zambesi.

Taken together, they show a concept of the world broad enough, and deep enough in time. At least when, in your *high-school years, the dean of what was to be your college scanned them, he said, with a chuckle, "I think we'll have to have this boy with us." Yet I suspect when you get back from this first tour of duty in the Far East, you'll find this picture that the bookshelves make vastly outgrown.*

For you've been serving with an outfit that uses books on a grand scale to send forth shafts of clear American light. Not that the works selected are all about our country, but they are chosen, as I understand it, to be consonant with our purposes abroad as well as at home. There are over a hundred and sixty USIA center libraries in some sixty countries. They contain, I'm told, about three million books, of which some nine hundred are translated into forty different tongues. And, just as at home, books are lent free of charge, and from open shelves. Not only are there bookmobiles in many lands, but small collections travel into remote corners of the globe by mule-back or by river barge as well. A kind of quiet guerilla warfare in "the battle of men's minds" of which you write.

Our giant arsenal is, of course, in Washington. On holidays there, in earlier years, that was the spot you always elected in which to wait while I did business in this federal department or that. I would return to find you happily holed up in piles of volumes called forth from the library's fathomless depths. You felt, even then, the glory of an institution, of a country, where one can summon up any idea in print, however controversial, however inimical indeed, to study it and question it and find the truth about it, in the large hushed calm that there prevails.

WHEN the famous British writer, H. G. Wells, had been shown through the Library of Congress, had gazed on priceless treasures behind glass, and wandered among shelves housing millions of books, he turned to the chief librarian at last and demanded:

"Why, with all this, doesn't it think?"

The question was a challenging one, asked by no other of the million-odd annual tourists who tramp the Library's marble halls, goggle at the book bound in human skin, the book smaller than a postage stamp, or at the Gutenberg Bible for which was paid a queen's ransom. But, within its stately cranium, the Library of Congress *does* think. In fact, it can think faster, and about more subjects at once, than any other organization you can turn to. It is the most thoughtful branch of the United States government— whether you mean slow deep thoughts or the quick and practical kind. Its business is information, and no commercial concern more efficiently or promptly delivers a tremendous volume of goods to its customers. The first served of these are more than five hundred Congressmen, nine Supreme Court justices and almost two hundred government agencies located in the national capital.

Thus, if a Congressman is making a speech and needs

a certain book, he has but to hand the name of it to a page boy and it will be immediately located on the shelves of the greatest book pile on earth, put on a conveyor belt under First Street from the Library to the Capitol, and delivered into the speaker's hand. Does Congressman Blank need statistics on sugar-beet production by tomorrow morning? His Library will find him exactly what he needs and it will be waiting for him on his desk by the time he gets down to the House Offices. Does the Senator want to inform himself irrefutably on mandates? The Library will get him up a complete bibliography on the subject, or abstract or copy excerpts from every latest significant work, and line his room with selected volumes. In short, it can and will read books *for* the Congressman and give him digests of them on which he can rely.

Gluyas Williams once drew a cartoon of a Congressman who had wandered into the Library of Congress reading room—whereupon all the staff fainted at the unexpected sight. Certainly they would be dismayed if he wasted his time in thumbing the millions of index cards and ordering up book after book in the hope of finding some kernel of fact he needed. For that would mean that he had lost faith in the Library's Legislative Reference Service, which saves Congressmen hours and months of time.

And don't think Congressmen don't use it. Each year Congress sends some seventeen thousand research requests to its wonderful library. Thousands and thousands of books are sent to them on loan. Many Congressional committees maintain unceasing research in study rooms reserved for them in the beautifully equipped new Annex building, where specialists on everything from cartels to coffee beans stand ready to help them.

Busy as Congress is in passing laws, it is far outclassed in volume of production by the forty-eight law factories of the separate states. How can a Congressman or Supreme Court judge keep posted on all this legislation? The Library of Congress takes care of that. Periodically it places on the desk of each Congressman and Justice a leaflet abstract of the new State laws. Similarly, all the latest information on postwar problems and planning rains down on official blotters from the same tree of knowledge.

The Library of Congress was far from my mind as I sat in the Supreme Court on the historic twenty-third of April, 1945, listening to the first decision it had ever rendered on a treason case—that of an American citizen who had been approached by Nazi saboteurs landed on our coast from a submarine in 1942. The majority decision read by Mr. Justice Jackson not only spared the accused but it protected you and me and our descendants from those who cry "Treason!" without the proof demanded by the Constitution. As the Justice read on, I listened in amazement not at his knowledge of Blackstone and John Marshall but at his wealth of citation from such varied writers as Montesquieu, Moses, Benjamin Franklin, James Wilson, George Mason, Samuel Johnson, Thomas Paine, and Stephen Vincent Benét. Later, I learned that the Supreme Court had turned to the Library of Congress to search the whole literature of treason and loyalty, not only as seen by governments and lawyers but by poets and philosophers, for the Library is a deep well of the wisest thoughts of men, and truth lies at the bottom.

When the United States went to war after Pearl Harbor, the big library was mobilized too. While the Nazis were burning their books, destroying so much that was good in German culture, the Congressional library was doing much more than treasuring Heine's *verboten* poetry and Thomas Mann's democratic defiance; through private agents all during the war it continued to buy up the documents of the Nazi government both public and secret. These were smuggled to neutral countries and flown to Washington. Moral filth and literary trash they may be, but they constituted a valuable record for the policing of Germany, and an indictment of war criminals of unparalleled completeness. Again, latest discoveries of German chemists concerning certain drugs, such as the sulfonamides, published where we couldn't get at them (as the Nazis supposed) were whisked unseen out of the country and brought to the Library of Congress, where they saved us months of research and thousands of American lives. A section of one of the great war agencies, organized under the Library's roof, answered requests for information ranging from the dissolution of marriages under the Nazi code to the operations of Soviet submarines under ice. The Army received invaluable aid in the bombing of Germany and Japan from the Congressional map collection, and the Chinese Air Forces turned to it for a precise knowledge of China which they themselves did not have.

For you never know what remote item in the vast

mausoleum of print may become of vital need. Certain shelves for forty years had been groaning under the voluminous weather reports of a far-off country having some of the heaviest rainfall in the world. Perhaps few or even no calls had ever been made on this material—until about 1942. Then all at once the United States Army took an intense interest in these reports; every detail of them constituted pearls of information beyond price except in American lives. For the country was Burma, and suddenly the whole strategy of a campaign was conditioned by the immediate availability, right in Washington, of those records that had so long seemed dead weight.

When the United Nations Conference agreed to meet in San Francisco, Uncle Sam's librarians collected and rushed to the coast a special library for use of the delegates, covering such subjects as mandates, treaty ports, war criminals, cartels, plebiscites, famines, postwar planning, and the Polish and Syrian questions. Not to mention incomparable atlases and dictionaries of everything from Arabic and Russian to Finnish and Chinese. For, if anything is international in our national setup, it is our Library; knowledge admits no boundaries.

This country first voted it a library by act of Congress in 1800. Something more than five thousand books were housed at that time in a room in the new Capitol building. In the War of 1812 the British set fire to it, and, as a horrified British soldier wrote home, "a noble library" was consumed in the flames. To form a nucleus for a new Congressional library, Thomas Jefferson sold the nation his personal collection of 6,487 volumes. It was probably the best in the country on government, history, economics, science, and philosophy—just what Congress needed. Yet it was not purchased without loud outcries that it was "atheistical," and that, at an average of $3.69 a volume, the ex-President was robbing the taxpayers. Today what is left of Jefferson's library, a couple of thousand volumes, after the Capitol's disastrous fires of 1825 and 1851, is considered priceless.

The Librarian of Congress is appointed by the President, just like a Cabinet officer. So in 145 years there have been but ten Librarians, for by tradition the appointment is for life. Only Jackson regarded the office as political spoils, removing the scholarly Watterston to make room for a henchman, Meehan. Regarded as a Southern sympathizer, Meehan was removed by Lincoln and too hastily replaced by Stephenson, who turned out to be a war profiteer. Just before his death Lincoln corrected his mistake, appointing Ainsworth Rand Spofford, one of the three truly great men who made the Library of Congress what it is.

With meager funds but tremendous enterprise, Spofford, in his thirty-three years of service, built up the Library from sixty-three thousand volumes (less than half as many as are found in the public library of my home town of Santa Barbara) to well over a million. People who called to see this dignified, tall bookworm were apt to find him surrounded by toppling mounds of books for which no place could be found in the cramped quarters. Yet he could dive into the pile anywhere and pull out the very volume required. Spofford it was who ceaselessly dinned into Congress the need for a separate building. Wild alternatives were proposed—one of them to stack the books in the dome of the Capitol! But at last the great Main Building was constructed, across the street from the Capitol, in the ornate style of the Paris Opera House, and there at last the vast collection Spofford had built up found living space. He himself resigned, then, in favor of a younger man.

If Spofford made the Library of Congress a big one, Herbert Putnam, who served from 1899 to 1939, not only quintupled it but made it systematic—methodical in its plan of purchase, exhaustive in the fields appropriate to the national library, and orderly in its arrangement. In his time the library again overflowed its bounds, and Congress built the Annex just behind the Main Building.

When Archibald MacLeish was appointed Librarian by Franklin Roosevelt in 1939, critics feared that because he was a poet he might be impractical. But MacLeish, with a long business experience, proved to be as effective a Librarian as Congress ever had. A vast treasure house of intellectual energy was already under his hand; he it was who, with the collaboration of department heads, mobilized the library for war. He fought for and obtained better salaries for its faithful scholars and servants. He gave special attention to the intricate mechanical workings of microfilming and efficient photostating, sound-recording, printing and binding.

Early in 1945 MacLeish resigned, to accept a post in the State Department, and President Truman, in June 1945, appointed Dr. Luther Evans, an "old hand" around the place. Dr. Evans is a Texas farm boy whose education began in the one-room, one-teacher Cedar Grove schoolhouse, but his brilliant mind carried him to teaching positions at New York University, Dartmouth, and Princeton. He came over in 1939 from the Historic Records Survey of the W.P.A. to be director of the Legislative Reference Service of the Library of Congress. No appointment to the most distinguished librarian position in the land was ever less opposed in the Senate, for Dr. Evans was obviously the ideal man for the job.

A few years before the outbreak of World War II, the Library of Congress overtook its two greatest rivals, the Bibliothèque Nationale in Paris and the British Museum, so that it is probably now numerically the largest in the world. True, only some seven million of its titles are books and pamphlets. But there is an almost equal number of manuscripts and rare unpublished documents, either in original form or photographed from other collections all over the world. Then, too, the human race is endlessly perpetuating its wisdom—and folly—in newspapers, motion pictures, photographs, and phonograph records. And all these the Library of Congress assiduously collects, no less than published books, until its total holdings run to twenty-three million items. It is still growing, at the rate of two and a half million a year! For less than twenty years more there will be storage room in the new Annex building, regarded as the last word in convenience, lighting, and air-conditioning (for the sake of the books, more than the readers). Then it too will be chockablock.

Without attempting to be the exhaustive repository of every subject, the Library of Congress is stronger than any other in the country in law, political science, and government documents both of our own and of foreign powers. Appropriately, it is richest in American history and literature. It is unsurpassed in the field of aeronautics, with twenty-five thousand titles. It has the largest collection of books in Russian and about Russia outside the U.S.S.R. Except in the Orient there is no rival to its collection of Chinese and Japanese books. Not of interest to specialized scholars only are these *orientalia*. Information on Japan and China was patiently amassed, beginning years ago, by the Congressional librarians. Today experts in Oriental languages are ready to translate or digest any subject in these collections, for the use of the State Department, the Navy and Army, or scholars of the Far East. For before the Japanese entered Peking, patriotic Chinese removed from their ancient National Library the rarest manuscripts in it, and the oldest printed books in the world. These were then sent secretly to the Library of Congress for safekeeping, and there they were microfilmed before being returned.

By plane every day are delivered the daily papers of the leading cities of Latin America. For the Library has been foresighted in realizing the waxing importance in our affairs of our American neighbors to the south. It publishes, in English, guides to the laws and legal literature of Cuba, Haiti and the Dominican Republic, of Mexico, Colombia, and the Central-American states. The average *gringo* may not take the literature, painting, and music of our southern neighbors as seriously as his own, but the Congressional librarians do so. Eagerly they collect all that is finest in the culture of two continents dominated by the Spanish and Portuguese languages. The Hispanic Foundation, supported in part by private endowment, is set up within the framework of the Library of Congress, with superb rooms in the Main Building, and is constantly collecting, sorting, and interrelating every Hispanic cultural product.

A gift, too, by Elizabeth Sprague Coolidge, has enriched the already splendid Music Division of the Library. Her foundation includes an auditorium in the Main Building where significant premières of modern composers are often heard. Here too the finest chamber music is performed upon the historic Stradivari, the gift of Gertrude Clark Whittall. If it is America's folk music that interests you, you will find a vast collection on records here, made right in the cotton fields, on Indian reservations, or wherever the common man lifts his voice in song. In the Library's sound laboratory, the Library concerts are recorded, and our poets recite their poems for posterity.

The Library provides "talking books" which speak to the blind. These are outsize phonograph records, in large albums, of the best of books, read aloud for the sightless who borrow them. Brazil has asked for some, and they are now available in Portuguese. Naturally enough, the Library of Congress is sponsor and clearinghouse for the volunteer work being done all over the country, in transcribing books into Braille, the raised print for the blind.

The most precious possession any library can boast is a collection of unduplicated manuscripts. Most of us think of manuscripts as the original versions of published classics, for it is these that bring fancy prices at auctions. But they are slight in importance compared with manuscripts of books that have never been published. Such, for instance, are the state papers and private correspondence of past Presidents. These are housed in well-guarded rooms, and just to walk down the long aisles and read the titles—the papers of Thomas Jefferson, of Abraham Lincoln, of Woodrow Wilson, of George Washington, makes an American's heart beat faster. Were the bodies of these great men to lie there in state, you would not be so much in their presence as you are when among the records of their thoughts and deeds.

Rare manuscripts possessed by other libraries can be studied at leisure right in the Library of Congress, by means of microfilm which reduces the bulk of the original to a tiny space, so that it is possible to reproduce hundreds of newspapers and store them in less room than a housewife might require for her winter's preserves. Torrents of newsprint are thus daily reduced and congealed, and anyone wishing to research the microfilm files can sit before an enlarging machine and read off the newspaper type with less strain on his eyes than the original would cause. Thus you can review Horace Greeley's first editorial in the *New York Tribune* for April 10, 1841, or discover baby Skeezix on Uncle Walt's doorstep where he lay so many years ago. For the comic strips and even the want ads are reproduced, since such matters constitute history and social commentary—so reason the librarians—on life in these United States.

And, of course, in the Library of Congress there are also the books! They are *your* books, if you need them and cannot find them elsewhere. Save for the very rare and valuable, and for genealogy and local history, such volumes may be borrowed through your home-town public library if they cannot be located in your state libraries.

Knowledge can free us all, and all of it contained in Uncle Sam's great library belongs to each of the more than one hundred and seventy million citizens of the United States. We all own an undivided share which is as big as our capacity to master it. Above all, the Library of Congress is there to be wise *for* us—wiser and more effective than as individuals we could hope to be. It is our great bank of free thought, on which statesman and citizen may limitlessly draw.

Arlington—
Where Sleep the Brave

🙢

I will not say very much by way of preface to the following pages. They take us to a presence in which silence is most fit. It is that of our most honored American, and the least known. If there is any Valhalla in which he now finds himself, there he must meet with others like himself, interred as symbolically in other countries. Surely there would be fellowship among such soldierly shades. So that it is not in his Americanism, after all, that his greatness lies, but in his humanity. May that, in time, become the common uniform of all!

THE most sacred ground in America is a few square feet of Virgina soil just across the Potomac from the city of Washington. More hallowed than any battlefield or monument, more revered than any relic or document, however historic, this spot has the power to unite the love and devotion of us all. For here, upon what was once part of the estate of Robert E. Lee, rests in honored glory a soldier greater than even he—"an American soldier known but to God."

To the tomb of the Unknown Soldier come every year more than two million pilgrims. On the day that you are reading these words, some five thousand will visit this shrine in Arlington National Cemetery. And tomorrow there will be another five thousand, rain or shine, and tomorrow and tomorrow. On Memorial and Armistice Days, as the heart of the nation swells with loving gratitude, fifteen thousand or more pour through Arlington's ten gates. Not to the Soldier alone do they come to pay homage, but to the multitude of his comrades in arms who sleep in the leafy acres around him. For those who lie in Arlington live still in our history, as any man does who gives his life for his country.

But Arlington is not a Hall of Fame. In the great democracy of death, generals and admirals rest beside privates and seamen. Together they represent service in all the wars ever fought to keep the United States of America whole and free. There are graves, only a few but precious, of men who fought in the Revolution. Here and there, too, is newly turned earth, the flowers still fresh upon it.

Yet you never walked in a cemetery that has so little grief in it. A greater emotion gives radiance to the sunlight. The only shadows are of the ancient trees, elms and oaks, magnolias and dogwoods whose petals, in their season, drift quietly to the grass. Despite whatever carnage and agony brought many of these men in the end to lie here, a shining peace prevails, visible and eloquent. It renders, to the thoughtful visitor, their united testimony that their sacrifice was worth while. So that, in Arlington, there is no horror, only glory.

By many a strange turn of fate did Arlington, once a forested wilderness, come to be the final sanctuary of our illustrious dead. It is part of six thousand acres deeded by Governor Berkeley of Virginia in 1669 to a ship's captain, as return for bringing in a fresh load of colonists. The captain promptly traded this land for six hogsheads of tobacco. And so it kept changing hands, more or less in speculation, until in 1778 it passed into the possession of John Parke Custis, son of Martha Washington by her first husband. He began to work it seriously as a plantation, and it was his son, George Washington Parke Custis, who in 1802 began to build Arlington House, which today you still see, shining out upon the forested heights of the Virginia shore.

Its lofty portico of white columns was fondly believed

by its builder to reproduce the temple of Theseus at Athens, but it looks to our eyes just what it is, and ought to be— the typical "old Southern mansion," fit scene for the wedding, in 1831, of young Lieutenant Robert Edward Lee to the owner's daughter, Mary Ann Randolph Custis. In time she inherited mansion and plantation, and here she and her husband were living happily when the storm clouds of the Civil War gathered. From here, one April day in 1861, Lee rode over the Potomac, at a call from the War Department, and there heard himself offered the command of the Union Armies. To answer either way was heartbreak. Though, detesting slavery, Lee had freed all his slaves, though better than any Southerner he foresaw long and bloody struggle, yet he refused the offer. He could not, he said, draw his sword against his kin and neighbors. So he rode back, that warm spring night, to the house on the wooded height, filled with the heavy premonition that he was now to leave Arlington forever.

In two days, indeed, he was on his way to Richmond to offer that stainless sword to the state of Virginia. A month later Mrs. Lee and the children followed him south. Swiftly Union forces occupied Arlington—a possession essential in the defense of the capital, because of its commanding situation. Swiftly ancient trees came crashing down, as ground was cleared for powerful Fort Whipple (now Fort Myer, a permanent military post) and Fort McPherson, whose earthworks are still seen, though covered with trees. On the ploughed fields of the farm, McClellan, the great drillmaster, marched his raw recruits up and down. The lovely mansion echoed to the tramp of boots; looters had carried off many of its treasures.

Powerless to protect her home, Mrs. Lee in Richmond was none the less receiving notices of taxes due on Arlington. They were only twelve dollars a year, and she sent these few dollars by an emissary promptly. But they were refused at the county courthouse, on the illegal grounds that she must appear with them in person. As she would not enter so obvious a trap, the estate was at last put up at auction, for deliquent taxes. In January 1864 it was bought in by the United States Commissioners.

Vicksburg and Gettysburg had been fought and won, and the end of the conflict could be seen afar, but long was the road yet, and bloody. The hospitals of Washington were crowded with wounded, both Union and Confederate, and from them many, too many, came forth as dead. But Uncle Sam had no national cemeteries to receive them, until Abraham Lincoln in deathless words so assigned the battlefield of Gettysburg. It was Quartermaster General Meigs who first suggested to the President that Arlington be dedicated to this same hallowed use, and in June Secretary of War Stanton so authorized. But already "Taps" had sounded here over turned earth beneath the great old trees. Officially or not, the first soldier had been buried here a month earlier, Private William Christman of the 67th Pennsylvania Infantry. Soon the sad bugle blew again and again, over the Blue and the Gray alike. From the battlefields of northern Virginia alone were gathered the bones of 2,111 unknown Union soldiers, placed in a single grave.

But even the bloodiest war spends its last red drops. When it was all over, when General and Mrs. Lee too were gone, their eldest son and heir sued the United States government for recovery of his estate. His legal battle went on for years, till it reached the Supreme Court, which gave the Lees justice at last. Technically, Mr. Lee might have required the removal of all those buried on Arlington's slopes. But, with a gesture worthy of his name, he instead offered Arlington to the United States government, for the sum—modest even in those days—of $150,000, that those who lay there might rest in peace. In 1883 Congress paid the sum and accepted the deed. And in 1925 Arlington House itself was restored to its old gracious beauty, with many authentic mementos of the Lees and copies of their original furniture, so that today it is thronged with delighted visitors from hospitable morning till the set of the sun.

The acres around the old home, some four hundred of them, offer a final resting place not only to our heroes killed in action, but to any honorably discharged veteran, and his wife, and his minor children. For each is provided a simple headstone; where identity is known, the headstone is rounded; if unknown, it is flat; "Rebel" stones are pointed. Any grander monuments are erected at the expense of friends, organizations, or by some special act of Congress. But there are few "high-horse" statues here. Even General Pershing, by his wish, lies under a simple block. Rear Admiral Robert Peary, discoverer of the North Pole, is honored by a stone globe, put up by the National Geographic Society. Men of the Coast Guard are memorialized by a sea gull poised before a rocky pyramid. The victims of the battleship *Maine*, which blew up in Havana harbor in 1898, are remembered by the mast of their ship. Among all these monuments to the brave acts of men, there is one tribute to womanly compassion no less valorous; where rest the Army and Navy nurses in a grassy hollow, there stands a heroic figure to represent them all, smiling tenderly toward her sleeping sisters, as one who passes through her hospital ward.

The nation recognizes that some of its greatest servants never wore uniform, and so includes civilians of the highest offices; thus President Taft and Secretary of Defense Forrestal lie here. Foreign servicemen who die on duty while in Washington may also be received in Arlington, which explains the imposing monument to Sir John Dill. So too there came here the great Polish statesman and pianist, Paderewski. He died in this country after his native land had fallen victim to the Communists, and here he awaits the day of liberation for Polish democracy.

Dazzling white upon the brow of Arlington Heights gleams the Memorial Amphitheater, its Vermont marble sharp against the soft Virginia sky. On the marble benches of this open-air theater may be seated some four thousand persons, and another thousand in the stately Doric colonnade that surrounds it. Here it is that crowds press in for the Easter sunrise service and observances on Memorial and Armistice Days. And indeed many times a year do patriotic and civic and other groups meet here to pay honor to the nation's dead. Every president, since Wilson laid the cornerstone in 1915, has here bent his head in prayer.

The Amphitheater houses a chapel, a guardroom for the

sentries, and a trophy room. Here are displayed all the medals and decorations heaped upon the Unknown Soldier —the Congressional Medal, the Victoria Cross tendered by Britain, the Croix de Guerre offered by the French government, and so on through the long list of nations allied upon the side of freedom, to a war bonnet and *coup* sticks presented by Chief Plenty Coups on behalf of all the American Indian tribes.

It was on Armistice Day in 1921 that the Unknown Soldier was brought to this spot. Never were such precautions taken to establish the *lack* of identity. From each of the four American battlefield cemeteries in France had been selected a body known by uniform and equipment to be that of an American, while gunshot wounds proved death in battle, and a total absence of papers or marks established anonymity. All four were brought to Châlons-sur-Marne and placed in identical caskets. Then, to the strains of a hymn from a military band, Sergeant Edward F. Younger (who also now rests at Arlington) walked slowly around the caskets, and at last laid solemnly upon one of them a wreath of red roses.

The U. S. cruiser *Olympia* bore the flag-draped casket, past the French fleet thundering salute, across the sea to Washington Navy Yard. By caisson it was transferred to the rotunda of the Capitol, where presidents have lain in state, and for two days a stream of visitors paid it honor. At eight-thirty on the morning of Armistice Day, Washington heard the first salvos of the minute guns from Fort Myer, which never ceased fire, at sixty-second intervals, for the five hours of ceremony that followed.

At the Capitol formed the procession which was to accompany the Unknown Soldier to Arlington—an escort of cavalry, a detachment of sailors, a platoon of infantry, and horse-drawn machine-gun troops. Slowly up Pennsylvania Avenue moved the rumbling caisson, the casket under its flag of stars enclosing the secret and inviolable identity of the one who is so many. Over the Francis Scott Key Bridge, through Fort Myer where the thundering guns rocked the chill air, wound the cortege. And now into the Amphitheater moved the clergy and choir led by the chief chaplain, all the highest brass and braid led by General Pershing, the diplomatic corps, the Cabinet members. The casket was borne by Army and Marine sergeants and Navy torpedo men around the colonnade and upon the stage—all the audience standing. At eleven-fifty the President and his lady entered and were seated; the Marine Band struck up "The Star Spangled Banner," and the Chief of Chaplains pronounced the invocation. The trumpet blast, at noon precisely, sounded "Attention" three times. Then for two minutes the vast concourse stood in silence.

The speeches, the hymns, the anthems, the commitment to the catafalque, where the casket rests forever upon soil gathered from the American battlefields in France, the reverent laying of wreaths, the ultimate benediction, the slow bugle notes of "Taps," the three salvos, crashing and final, of the minute guns—at last they are over, and the crowd disperses. Now there is only the snapping of the flag upon the pole, the rhythmic tramp of the sentry, up and down, all day, all night, in sun or storm, the never-ending vigil. Throughout the years this sentry has walked his post by a military clockwork of paces and turns that takes exactly one minute to execute, and exactly every hour the guard is changed, the Tomb saluted again. All the sentries are volunteers; proudly they claim that "this is the Number One guard post of the nation."

Day after day come dignitaries, foreign and domestic, to lay each his official tribute at the Tomb. On my last visit I watched such a ceremony, complete with ambassador, silk hats, dress swords, and battery of news cameras. The color guard was turned out for this, performing its faultless and dramatic evolutions. A bit later another group arrived with a wreath—some Boy and Girl scouts from a small town in Maryland. There were no cameras, no silk hats, but again the color guard turned out in full, again sounded the sergeant's bark, the thump and clash of arms presented. The boy and girl who carried the wreath had been picked not for their looks but—as should be—for their merit badges; together they offered their tribute as humbly as a prayer. Both were awed, visibly. So was I. When the youngsters had filed away, when the last notes of "Taps" had floated off over the Tomb, when only the sentry remained at his endless pacing, eternity was so silent you could hear a whitethroat sparrow singing his Sweet, sweet, sweet! "Sweet and fitting"—*dulce et decorum* —"is it to die for one's country."

Lee's Greatest Victory

Here I give you some pages about a great American who had to haul down his flag. We like to say that, as a nation, we have never lost a war. A campaign, yes; many of our campaigns have failed, whether through bad management, or inferiority in numbers and equipment, or even because our allies wanted the battling to stop. But a war—no. Americans never emerged from one totally defeated, except once.

And that was when the South lost, in complete exhaustion of every sort of supply, and of irreplaceable manpower. So it took Americans utterly to defeat Americans. Even so, the winning side might not have won but for superiority of numbers and money and material. And it is generally agreed that the greatest strategist of that war was on the side that lost.

I wish that the peoples of the earth who think of us as an arrogantly unconquerable nation might know how he, and many other Southerners, behaved after the surrender.

For they were very American in their defeat. Soldiers returned quietly to their homes—if these were still standing. Women bound up the wounds; their growing children triumphed over poverty. Grace and pride and intellect somehow survived. The spirit of the South's own and real reconstruction owed most to the example of its greatest hero, Robert Edward Lee.

Yet (do you know, Mark?) when I first wrote and published the following account of him after Appomattox, I received a barrage of furious letters from professional Southerners. For I had shown that if there was anything of which Lee sternly disapproved, it was that element in the South that still belligerently waved the Confederate banner. He had no use for the self-styled "unreconstructed Rebel." The war over, he wanted hate well buried. Indeed, even in the heat of battle, he had seldom referred to "the enemy" but spoke of the Union forces as "those people."

Now, in the war of ideas to which you summon me, this noble restraint is one to be remembered. If there is any clear-cut enemy we all should be fighting, it is the ranks of hate and fear. So you young people in the foreign service go about showing in alien places the best of our native courtesy and tolerance. You would bring, I think, a smile to the tired lips in the white beard of the great gentleman from Virginia.

O UT of the farmhouse parlor at Appomattox, General Robert Edward Lee walked erect and unflinching. He had just surrendered the remnant of his army and accepted total defeat. When he closed the door behind him, the career of the greatest American soldier ended. Now, as he stood at the top of the steps, he gazed with unseeing eyes at that April day (Palm Sunday) in 1865. What he saw was the wrecked hopes and fortunes of the seven million white population of the Confederate States. The south wind brought him not the perfume of pinesaps in the woods where his men were encamped, but the stench of war and the unheard anguish of a million of its orphans and widows. Suddenly he smote his gloved hands together twice—the gesture of a man who has done all in human power and found it not enough.

Under the crushing double burden of defeat and responsibility, Lee descended the steps of the McClean farmhouse as Traveller, his faithful gray, was led to meet him. Thoughtfully he adjusted the silvery forelock over the bridle band. When he had swung into the saddle, he saw that General Grant had come out upon the steps. The two men raised their hats, one to the other, in silence; all that lay between them had been said, and well said. What lay ahead for Robert Lee was beyond words.

As Lee rode back to his lines, the men in gray crowding up to him read the truth in his careworn face. The noble head, whose hair and beard had turned in the four years of conflict to snowy white, was held high. But his voice broke as he told the frankly weeping veterans that all was over. *Go home*, he advised each who asked him; *plant a crop, obey the laws.*

Robert E. Lee had surrendered only his military forces to a stronger power; he had not yielded the fate of the South to despair. The war was over, and with it must go all its hatred, pride, and anger. Carefully from *General Orders* n. 9, the farewell to his army prepared for him, he struck out a paragraph which he feared might fan the embers, so thoroughly deleting it that we no longer know what were the inflammatory words. Then, and for the rest of his life, he refused to revive the issues that had died with the million men who had died for them.

By the surrender terms, Lee's men were free to find their way to their homes—if standing. To weed-high fields and hungry children. The sorrows of the Southern people, that even years later would keep Robert E. Lee pacing the floor at two in the morning, were a vast inundation on which they were all at sea. And because he had led them through four bloody years to this disaster, because they loved him still and looked to him more than to any other man living as their undiminished ideal, he was still their leader.

Not till the last Confederate soldier had started on his weary march homeward did the greatest of them turn Traveller's head in that direction. Accompanied by a few officers, he rode for three days toward Richmond through all the troubling sweetness of a Virginia spring. So much had he loved Virginia that for her fair sake he had turned against the Union. He who hated slavery and had freed his slaves, who considered secession as bald revolution and madly rash, had yet thought of Virginia first and defended her to the last. He could not, he had explained simply, draw his sword against his birthplace. Virginia itself was a cause, Blue Ridge and Shenandoah, Piedmont and Tidewater— names like haunting notes of music, notes to make a chord, chords that make a melody. For her he had fought, taking her sons with him. But when General Lee unbuckled his sword in his Richmond house, he laid it down forever. He made peace in his heart and set his face toward the future, dark as it was.

Edmund Ruffin, the rabid secessionist who proudly fired the first shot against Fort Sumter from Morris Island, blew out his brains when the Confederacy fell. Other Virginians left the state, to become morose and useless expatriates abroad. But Lee declared, "Now more than at any time Virginia and every other state in the South needs us." A group of his old soldiers begged him to come to Tennessee where they could "protect" him. "Would you have your general run away and hide?" he answered them.

His status was the same as that of tens of thousands who had followed him—a paroled prisoner of war. But when President Johnson extended a general amnesty to the former Confederates, it expressly excluded Lee. The privilege was offered him, however, to make special application for pardon. Gravely Lee considered this. So to bow to authority would be to set an example to millions of Southerners who might think it right to keep alive a spirit of resistance. But at this moment a movement was started to indict Robert E. Lee and other Confederates for treason against the United States. Lee hesitated. To ask for pardon now might seem to flinch before a trial. He took his problem straight to his old adversary General Grant, who replied that, as a prisoner honoring his parole, General Lee could not be indicted for treason. So Lee, fearless even of humiliation, applied for pardon. For this, bitter die-hards (most of them not soldiers) were to pursue his memory beyond the grave with reproaches. But untold numbers of Southerners reasoned that if their idolized leader could return in sincere loyalty to the Union, they could follow him in peace as they had in war. No victory that Grant ever won brought back to the Union so many brave and loyal hearts as this act of Lee's.

And Lee had reason to feel one with the veterans whom war had stripped. His beautiful home at Arlington had been confiscated by the government for taxes, its furnishings looted by civilians. His investments had dwindled. With his invalid wife and several daughters, he was living in a cottage that had been put at his disposal by a generous friend. Such kindly offers of help were many. One English nobleman invited him to be a guest his life long. "I cannot desert my native state," Lee answered, "in the hour of her adversity."

Bitterly his daughter Mary remarked that the South would give her father anything—except what he wanted most, the chance to earn his living. This speech reached the ears of the trustees of a forlorn little institution in Lexington, Virginia. Washington College had always been small, though with a history, under various names, dating back to 1749. War's end found it looted of library and laboratory equipment, with many of its buildings too dilapidated for use, others garrisoned by Federal troops, and only forty-five students and four professors on the roster. When the trustees met after Appomattox, the simplest course might have seemed to close the school's doors. Instead, they voted to struggle on, borrowing money to repair buildings and pay salaries and, quite without his knowledge, elected to the presidency of the college the noblest living American.

All they could offer Robert E. Lee was $1500 a year, a house to live in when one could be got ready, and one-fourth whatever tuition could be raised. But Lee saw more in the offer than the small opportunity for himself. To him the gravest loss of the South, after the lives of her soldiers, was in her cultural and moral values. For four years, her finest young men had been deprived of higher education; now the country was filled with veterans trained only to fight, or to live in a world that was over. Teaching them, he might teach the defeated Confederacy the hard lessons to be learned. Friends pointed out that he could easily find a place in a more famous institution. Lee shook his head; to rebuild from ruins was the task of all his people. So it was that through the blazing heat of September, 1865, Lee headed westward on Traveller, for Lexington. He could not know, as he breathed the red dust of the roads and sadly noted the abandoned fields and fire-gutted houses, how the news of his intention sent a thrill of hope and resolve throughout the South.

Washington and Lee, as the college now proudly calls itself, has grown since Traveller's rider first saw it, but the new buildings are hidden by the old ones marshaled still on the crest of the hill, much as Lee used to dispose his batteries in defense. Yet unlike the grimly battlemented Virginia Military Institute, whose campus adjoins it, Washington and Lee had then as now the look of peace on its soft-red bricks and lofty white pillars. This, then, was to be Lee's last home, the scene of his last battles—against poverty, exhaustion, and demoralization, those guerilla foes still to be fought after war is over.

The very name of Robert E. Lee brought to Washington College an immediate increase in enrollment, which rose, presently, from forty-five to four hundred. Of these many were bearded veterans, some determined to make up for time lost in war, some war-hardened, hard-drinking, spoiling to start trouble with the town boys, the Federal garrison, the newly liberated Negroes, and the carpetbaggers. General Lee, the West Pointer, the stickler for discipline, faced them with a standard even harder and higher than the military. "We have but one rule here, and that is that every student must be a gentleman."

To emphasize that he was training men not as fighters but workers, Lee deliberately walked out of step with the band, whenever his students marched with those of V.M.I. He abolished formal inspections and punishments, and instituted instead an honor system. It included unswerving attendance at classes, the highest personal morals, courtesy unflagging, respect for property, and submission to civil authority. Above all Lee's honor system meant hard work, for almost every boy in college, he knew, was there at extreme personal sacrifice by some war-impoverished family. Work and save, work and save! So he preached, and so he practiced.

Though president, he had to be his own secretary, his own superintendent of buildings and grounds. He, who hated paper work and had kept five secretaries busy in the army, toiled alone in that little office, so modest as to be almost bleak, in the basement of the chapel, answering by hand all the college correspondence, acting too as an employment bureau for the students. He personally supervised the construction and maintenance work. Nothing roused the old president's ire like waste. Every rail from a tumbled-down fence must be saved, every scrap of paper used over and over; worn-out tools must be mended. Except on ceremonial occasions the president dressed in threadbare clothes, perhaps because so many of his students could dress no other way.

Nor must the South merely salvage what she could; she must prepare for new opportunities. Washington College had formerly specialized in Latin, Greek, rhetoric, and pure mathematics—just such a training as Lee himself had had, the training for an *ante-bellum* life of cultivation and leisure. Those days were gone; the trend of the times was scientific. So, as fast as funds became available for new professorships, Lee added courses in civil engineering, agricultural chemistry, and modern languages. His keen eyes, peering into the future, perceived the coming of increasingly close relations with Latin America, and he urged the study of Spanish upon his boys. Success came to meet this courage. Cyrus McCormick, in answer to one of Lee's few personal solicitations, gave $10,000 to this little fortress of hope and learning in his native Shenandoah. Other contributions followed; men believe in those who believe in themselves.

Handsome offers came to Lee personally. He might perhaps have been president of the Chesapeake and Ohio Railway. He could certainly have drawn down a salary of the then munificent sum of $10,000 a year in the Knickerbocker Insurance Company, with only the lightest of duties required of him. But Lee would not desert his "boys." His personal influence with the student body was so great that, composed of discordant elements though it was, it united in obedience to his wishes as law. The whisper that "Marse Robert" wouldn't allow something was enough to quash any mischief.

When a horse thief was caught in Lexington, he would have been lynched if President Lee had not appeared on the scene in time. A Negro and a white boy quarreled; the Negro shot his adversary in the leg. The students were prepared to hang the assailant when Lee rushed to the scene, demanding that the law be allowed to take its course. The Negro's life was saved, and, equally important, the students were saved from committing a crime. One can easily imagine what the idol of the Southern people would have to say about Southern senators who filibuster anti-lynching legislation to death. Or his scorn for persons who

think themselves too good to shake a Negro by the hand.
It is a certainty that Robert E. Lee did so when he met an
old colored friend.

The South today is filled with monuments to Lee the
soldier; one marks his resting place in the crypt of the old
college chapel where he was laid on October 14, 1870. But
his greatest monument is invisible. It is the example he
set not only the South in his day but the whole country
for all time, of a Christian soldier who went onward in
faith, humility, courage, and justice in times more bitter
and disheartening than the war itself. Out of defeat he
wrested victory. "We failed," he said of the lost cause,
"but in the good providence of God, apparent failure often
proves a blessing. It is history that teaches us to hope."

Discovering America

Appomattox and Arlington, the monuments of the capital and the missions of California—they are all "sights," the goal of tourists both native and foreign. But behind them lies the land itself, and into that, like all happy American families, we have loved to go journeying. The best of such trips have been those with you, Mark, at the wheel, not only because you drive with a care to match your daring, but for the zest of your informed companionship. Even over washboard lane or sandy ruts you'll navigate (your brothers chuckling at your enthusiasm), to reach the site of some particularly bloody massacre or the spot, empty now but for the wind in the sagebrush, where Apaches fired a train of covered wagons.

I wondered, then, where you and Alice might be wandering, in that car you had sent out to Cambodia, austerely bare of chrome but equipped for the tropics. Then came a letter telling of your first weekend free of duties. "We went down to Kep on the Gulf of Siam, for the Cambodian

New Year. *The ocean was as warm as bathwater, and you could swim 'way out and still touch bottom; we swam at night, with a sliver of silver moon above the palms fringing the shore, and every stroke made a dazzling phosphorescence.*

"Next day we drove up into the hills in back of the beach, and into the jungle. On each side of the road was a mass of bamboo, thorn bushes, ferns, and over all towering trees with high thin roots spreading up from the ground and, suspended from lofty branches, twisted ropes of evil-looking vines. On the leaves everywhere were insects—great black and white ants with fierce jaws, brilliant butterflies, midges, gnats, beetles. Sometimes far off, sometimes quite near, we heard the weirdest bird calls. As the road wound higher we caught glimpses of the Gulf of Siam glittering blue beneath the trees, with the long brown mudflats stretching out to meet it. Here and there below us in the distant valley were small rectangular pepper plantations. Halfway up to the top of the mountain we came on the tracks of an elephant which must have passed only a little while before. . . ."

Now that's junketing! *I shall not see the jungle now, I suppose, nor the beach at Kep, any more than I'll really roll to Rio. Indeed, the savagery of our own highways nowadays has grown forbidding. But for twenty years I've gloried, like my fellow citizens, in the roads that every morning call you up and away, and into a country so great and grand that none of us can ever learn it all by heart. And it's all worth remembering. . . .*

W HEN I was small, not a half century ago, a "horseless buggy" came putt-putting down our street, dodging mudholes, about once a week. By the time I went to college, we had to quit that house because of the rush of traffic. Even a decade ago the United States could boast a car for every four persons in its population. Today Mr. and Mrs. America and Son and Sis are on the road more than ever; they are pushing out their horizons, and with new life and liberty are pursuing happiness on wheels.

But motoring, like any sport, requires skill. Not just skillful driving, though that is a first requisite, since your best insurance against trouble is to remember, through all the delights of speed and passing beauty, that the automobile is a lethal instrument. Yet there's more to wise motoring than smart or careful driving. That's enough, of course, for mere transportation from one place to another, but when you travel for pleasure, not business, you must put out of mind all thought of "making time on the road." To make time—a grand time, a time you'll never forget—on the shining network that crisscrosses America, is to make the most of the new and colored world through which you pass.

It happens to be my business, as a roving editor of

Reader's Digest, to do just this. I have to know what to look for, and how to look at it. And the more my wife and I journey into America, the deeper, we have found, you can go. We are all pilgrims on the road together, you and I and our vacationing children, and what some of us seek is the spirit of our country—its beloved smile, its ever-changing, never-failing friendliness, its lingering primeval beauty, its historic greatness—that, like a fresh wind rippling the flag, can lift the heart of the enlightened motorist.

Yet many a driver sees little more than the car ahead of him, the billboards to right and left, and such views as are labeled "scenic." His eyes, so keen to calculate the chances of passing the fellow in front, are untrained to see the Nature, the underlying story, even the obvious beauty, of what lies about him. What he talks about is the insolent behavior of other drivers; what he listens for is that stupid little rattle in the fender. He has lost what as a child, at least, he had—curiosity and wonder, those keys to discovery. For him the traffic is the only challenge, the four-lane highway the only possible route, and the one thing he will stop for is gas.

Bad habits can make dullards of us all. But anyone can practice expert motoring, whether at the wheel or not. We early taught our children how to get the most out of trips in the family car, and while teaching them we learned much ourselves. We taught them not to require distraction. The radio, for instance, we use only when the music is good, as an orchestration for beauty, or later in the day as a refreshment for road weariness. We learned that if one person is allowed to read a sign aloud, none of the others can escape the odious insistence of billboards. We found that family harmony was never more necessary or sweeter than in the close companionship within that tiny traveling home. And that, like all homes, it was the pleasanter for frequent exits from it, so that we stopped often to let young legs scamper, just as we two still stop and stroll, now and then, by a lake shore or beside a brook. Most of all we taught our boys to turn their eyes and thoughts away from themselves and out into the bright, passing world.

For that is the true freedom of the road—that release from self and home, office and school, work and habit which motoring uniquely gives. Walking's too slow, flying's too high, and the train is too confined for this particular rapture, this rush into the heart of things, which is motor wonder. It begins at your door, and will take you as far as you please—to Fairbanks, Alaska, or to an old manor house, a fern-hidden cave, a covered bridge, an epic oak, in some unexplored corner of your own county.

If you're going farther afield, don't lug your local pride along. A lady from Vermont wrote a book about her trip to California by car; the gist of it was that she wished she had never left home, and so did this reader. There are no redwoods in Maine, no brooks on the desert, no cozy quaintness in all the wide West—so forget them. I've known people from hilly and forested country who set out across Kansas with a groan, and blamed it all the way. But Kansas is beautiful; it has the widest arc of sky, the deepest sea of wheat, the cheeriest meadowlarks I know. Whenever I cross Kansas, I think of the old Santa Fe Trail that I am following, and when I see a cottonwood shining on the horizon I realize, better than in merely woodsy country, how precious is a tree. In each state, in all the great natural provinces of our country, there is an individual flavor— there are even odors of forest and marsh and field, sounds like chime of mission bells or chant of laboring Negroes, that belong to just that corner of America. In all patriotism, we owe each an ungrudging admiration.

With this open mind, bring too a flexible purpose. Plan your trip carefully, of course—and then be willing to scrap your plans at the crook of the beckoning road. Once, on my way from Williamsburg to Washington, I saw a sign that, pointing up a sandy lane, said "To the Ferry." I believe in ferries, and so does my wife, so we took that lane, we took that ferry, and five others during a day that revealed to us the heart of Virginia's tidewater country, once the realm of planter princes. We discovered Colonial houses and gardens dreaming in forgotten serenity by the river; we ate soft-shell crabs and fresh strawberries where there was no one else to eat them. We talked with perch fishermen, colored children, stray dogs, and poked among mossy headstones honoring the first of great families, ending up, just when we were tired, at an unguessed inn as good as a wish come true. Which all supports my first rule of pleasure motoring: Never take a highway, if you can find a byway.

For only the byways will lead you deep into America. The highways will take you straight to the great known sights, and you'll want to see them, of course, but if you never take a hunch turning, you'll never find anything out for yourself. In wide-open Texas, which seems to hold no secrets, we followed an intuition to Castroville, an Alsatian village only an hour from San Antonio, a spot with one of the most stirring records of pioneering courage in America's frontier history—yet plenty of Texans do not know it to boast of. In Kentucky the same luck led us to Shakertown, a bit of the religious life of early America preserved in tranquillity, a settlement full of ingenious antiquities, where we spent the night at an inn with everybody out. A little sign by a Tennessee roadside told us nothing but "To Happy Valley," and the happiness we found there made one of the best days in our lives, for the winding road led us to a place that has not retrogressed from simpler times; the loudest sounds were songs of grosbeak and chat, a man calling to his plowhorse, the laughter of barefooted children in the brook, and the clack of a loom where a woman was weaving. There are happy valleys and historic villages in every state; the motorist has no sweeter rewards than the finding of them.

And you don't have to depend entirely on hunch and chance. We wouldn't think of driving off without the books we'll need on the back window shelf of the car. Since I am a naturalist, these include field guides to birds, trees, and flowers, but the volume that will double anybody's pleasure is the one about the state he is motoring in, from the American Guide Series. Forty-eight of these stretch across my library shelves, and marvelous reading they make, at home or upon the road. Titled each simply by the state's name, they are put out by various publishers —your library or bookseller can get them for you. Each of them follows the roads of its state, mile by mile, town by town, telling what's to be seen in each and what events happened there, hinting of an ancient church up this lane, an historic mansion down that one, and making lively for you even a sleepy crossroads by the tale of some Civil War skirmish or Indian raid.

Other books can guide you into America, too. There's a series on its mountain ranges and their life, another on its rivers, and the American Guide Series contains volumes on cities from Key West to Portsmouth, from New York to San Francisco. But some of the best reading you'll pick up right on the spot; at "The Hermitage," in Tennessee, for instance, I collected books on Andrew Jackson not easily found elsewhere, and have gathered local histories and helpful pamphlets at "Monticello," "Mount Vernon," Tombstone, and Marblehead.

For from coast to coast, on turnpike and in tavern, in ancient courthouse or on village green, this land is one richly colored broidery of stories, and they all add up to the history of America. That is, above all, an epic of westward exploration. This people, we Americans, went west—hewing and fighting and pushing our way—by the Natchez Trace and the National Road, the Wilderness Trail, the Oregon Trail, the Old Spanish Trail. And today you and I can follow those ghostly and heroic paths. They'll be paved now, mostly; sometimes they'll be four-lane highways; roaring old U.S. 66 through New Mexico is really the Santa Fe Trail; U.S. 30 through Wyoming parallels much of the Pony Express route, and the Butterfield stagecoach lumbered along, dodging Apache arrows, on what is now U.S. 80 in Arizona. Do you want Daniel Boone for a

leader? Take U.S. 25 East, through the Cumberland Gap,
and see him ahead of you cutting his way through primeval
brush, up over Clinch Mountain, past the Rockcastle, into
Blue Grass. Or will you follow Lewis and Clark, as we did
one memorable summer? We picked up their trail at
Three Forks, Montana, and crossed the Continental Divide
with them at the Lemhi Pass—no highway here, but only
grassy ruts through the mariposa lilies under the giant
pines.

For, next to the gas in your tank, the most important
thing to take along when you motor is your imagination.
This will be fired by a little fireside travel at home before
you start, so that you'll understand what you're seeing
when you look at it. And the chances are that, when you
get home, you'll want to read those books all over again,
now that you've been to the scenes of the stories. While
you're there, don't be afraid to ask questions of the local
inhabitants; they'll be proud to tell you. Everybody in the
great Northwest, for instance, knows about Sacajawea, the
girl guide of Lewis and Clark, just as everyone down in the
bayou country of Louisiana is glad to talk to you about
the patriotic pirate, Jean Lafitte. Ask the town librarian;
she'll be a fund of accurate information; an oldster who's
lived there all his life will love to take out for you his
well-polished memories, as the druggist in Virginia City
did for us.

All this, of course, takes time—the time of your life. To
stop, look, and listen, to wonder and dream along the way,
is to put your hand on the great beating heart of your
country. For knowledgeable motoring, if you're not ready

to stop on the way, you are not ready to start. The easy flight across the country, the scenes flashing by so fast they are gone before you saw them, the wind in your face, the light on the land—all this is glory, and the tingle in motoring. The road is your ribbon of adventure. But strung upon it are the memories you will treasure—that hour under the great elm by the bubbling spring, that ten slow minutes lost to churchyard peace by ivied walls, and the little while that you stood on the canyon's rim, in an immense silence, watching an eagle soar over the seas of aspen gold below you both. This, after all, is what you set forth to find—this, and what lies beyond the next curve in the road, and over the farther hill.

Rocky Mountain Roving

You'll see a lot more of this spinning globe, my son, than
I ever have, before you're through. It's a daily wonder to
me where they'll send you next, when you have finished
this tour of duty in Phnom Penh. In Army service you
managed to rove what part of the eastern states I had not
shown you, and once stationed in Bavaria you scouted out
its loveliest corners. Getting leave, your passion for the past
at its most romantical took you, with a couple of astonished
comrades in arms, across France and into Holland and over
the Channel, to motor through the bitter winds of a Scottish so-called springtime, all the way up to the Highlands.
And at Culloden you reached a goal of your young lifetime,
and suffered gloriously for the glorious fallen of so long
ago.

Here at home in California you are seized frequently by
an attack of what you've dubbed "the Western goes." Then
you must saddle whatever well-used car you happen to
own, and drive bucking out between our old stone gate-

*posts to follow some trail of which your reading gave you
scent. But there's one Western heaven you don't know.
You've never scaled the ramparts of our Rockies. So I put
in the pages that here follow to lure you back, some holiday
with Alice, to pioneer this heart of your own land.*

C OMING west over the old buffalo plains, you see at
last on the wide horizon what looks like a low
gleaming cloud. So it appeared to the first American who ever came to the mountains of Colorado, young
Lt. Zebulon Pike. But when, that day in 1806, he raised
his spyglass to it, he saw that the cloud was "a great peak"
—Pike's Peak, we call it now in his honor. And as he and
his little band toiled eagerly toward it, peak beyond peak
the Front Range of the Rockies reared higher, coming
nearer, coming clearer, swathed at the base in dark ever-
green forests and topped with the glitter of snows. Now
the Americans unfurled their flag, to snap proudly in the
wind from those cold heights, while all waved their hats
and shouted three cheers for the Rockies. And that is just
what you will want to do, when first you see that great
storm of frozen earth-waves rising in a long wall.

For what lies beyond it is your holiday, your green vacation in a region literally tops in America, since Colorado holds more high summits than any other state in the nation. Here is air so dry and pure it enters the lungs like rapture. Here is a wilderness welcoming with camp sites; here are ghost towns and live towns, and highways crisscrossing the Continental Divide by alpine passes. Here you can spend days knee-deep in wild flowers, hip-deep in singing trout streams. True that the foothills, even at 7000 feet where the slopes begin, are hot in summer, but mount another 1000 feet or more and you'll meet a freshening sparkle in the air. It's cool enough there in July for forests of Christmas trees to grow, and warm enough to picnic coatless among them. And the skies are mostly clear as a great blue bell, unless there breaks upon your untroubled head one of those hair-raising mountain thunderstorms—a tantrum soon over.

Capital of this Rocky Mountain empire is the high-hearted city of Denver, and you couldn't make a better beginning than here. Whether you come by train, plane, or motor, whether you hire a "drive-it-yourself" car or use the generous system of excursion buses provided, you can fill two or three weeks richly with travel from this town as base. Right around the busy city are 25,000 acres of playground wilderness, the Denver Mountain Park System, which includes Mt. Evans, climbed by the highest automobile road in North America. But Denver itself, mile-high and mountain-ringed, is one of the sights, from the U.S. Mint to the old-style state capitol, its dome glistering with gold leaf mined right here in Colorado. Some Denverites complain that their town has buried its rip-snorting past too deep under civic virtue and such cultural graces as symphonies under the stars and a summer theatrical season. But it's a male town still, with enterprise and politics in the air. And what air! So tingling you have trouble keeping your heels on the sidewalks. When F.D.R. asked Justice Douglas how to better the Supreme Court, the answer shot back, "Move it out to Denver!"

But most of us go to Colorado (and maybe over her borders into sagebrush Wyoming and sunburnt New Mexico) not for any city but to enjoy that spectacular western nature which is the prime adventure in America. So head out of Denver on the short freeway to Boulder and thence to Estes village and right into Rocky Mountain National Park, for if you never saw any more of Colorado than this you would still have tasted of its best. There are over 400 square miles of it, gemmed with lakes reflecting boughs and boulders, and laced with streams born but minutes ago from glacial ice and summer sun. In one eyeful you behold both white peaks against clear azure and a long valley brimming with lupine and gentian, larkspur and harebell, Indian pink and Indian paintbrush. And with the pride of the state, its columbine, here grown so big it seems like a garden runaway, eloquent, in its spurred and airy grace, of summer freedom.

Exercise at 9000 feet is at first as breath-taking as the scenery, but soon you'll climb trails with a zest you never knew you had in you. If you are a genuine hobnail, rope, and alpenstock mountaineer, you'll find forty-seven summits in the Park over 12,000 feet above sea level, with

Long's Peak (14,215 feet) as the outstanding challenge. To less ambitious eyes the Never-Summer mountains look just as noble from a seat on pine needles, and a car will take you right over them on the Trail Ridge Road. There above timber line, where the alpine flowers crouch before the planetary gales, you may gaze out over the Rockies as God made them—wild, grand, unspoiled, a sea of tossing whitecaps stretching away and away, world without end.

Some of the towns down there are right out of our favorite Westerns, and their history is epic. Gold was discovered around Denver in 1858, and the next year the prairies were streaked white with "schooners" bearing the legend *"Pike's Peak or Bust."* For sixteen years men were fevered by gold, as they prospected every gully and slope, undaunted by snow and avalanche, starvation, accidents, Utes and claim-jumpers. Though the easy pickings of gold gave out—dramatically or disastrously—luck held, for silver was suddenly found, and the Rockies went on a bigger and better spree. Towns like Leadville, Telluride, Aspen, Central City, Cripple Creek, Fairplay, and Ouray sprang up overnight, growing crazily along the windings of canyons or climbing beside the lode above timber line. In them all boom and bust (or, in miners' Spanish, *bonanza* and *borrasca*) followed the same pattern, as the price of gold and silver rose or fell, as veins "pinched out" or new strikes were made. In bonanza poor men like "Haw" Tabor and Thomas Walsh struck it rich in a matter of days, and could buy diamonds for their women folk, throw champagne and oyster banquets, build "opry" houses, and shower the actress of the moment with nuggets. Then, in borrasca, their fortunes would melt away as swiftly as they came. And when the roar of stamping mills, mine pumps, and hoisting works ceased, hundreds of citizens might take flight from a town in a day.

Such was the history of Central City, only forty miles west of Denver. Once it boasted that it was "the richest square mile on earth." By 1929 it was all but forsaken; the pulse of the mines was barely perceptible; the Teller House where mining kings had feasted was boarded up; the Opera House was shut in musty darkness. Unlocked one day in sheer curiosity, it revealed to some Denver enthusiasts a past still living. Under the dust showed lines of grace; whitewash could not hide the lovely murals; the chandelier kept in its prisms some gleam of the jewels and high notes of dead divas. It took three years, through the depths of the depression, to revive this sleeping beauty, but when at last the curtain rose on *Camille* with Lillian Gish, bonanza days were back. Now the Central City Opera Festival brings to life each summer some other classic—by Verdi or Mozart, by Shakespeare or Ibsen. Again the Teller House is crowded and its Gold Nugget Bar gay with revelers.

But you'll be hearing the call of "something lost behind the Ranges. Lost and waiting for you. Go!" You may go, climbing up over Rabbits Ears Pass, to Steamboat Springs, where yearly hundreds swirl in a square-dance contest. You may follow the rodeo season around, for almost every Rocky Mountain town, and many a working ranch, has its own; the biggest and showiest may be "Frontier Days" in Cheyenne, breezy and hospitable capital of Wyoming. Or you may pull up by a stream to rent a pan and sift the

gravels for gold—(no money back). But if, like me, you are
an incorrigible "saddle bum" of western motoring, you will
just sample such fun, and then roll on, taking what comes,
carefree as gypsies—on over Loveland Pass or Wolf Creek
Pass, over the Medicine Bow Mountains and the dreamy
Sangre de Cristos, stopping to peer fearfully into the depths
of the Black Canyon of the Gunnison, or to cross the Royal
Gorge on the highest suspensio.1 bridge in the world, where
you can watch the Denver and Rio Grande trains forging
along at the bottom like a child's toy. A week of such ad-
venturing, and your head will be in a happy whirl of snowy
summits, echoing gorges, roaring streams, and marching,
marching forests.

All the time, all the way, you are catching vivid glimpses
of Rocky Mountain nature. Those great trees, seemingly
dusted with moonlight, that look like the tidy blue spruce
on your home lawn *are* blue spruces, Colorado's state tree.
The ones with the pencil-slim outlines and somber foliage
are Engelman spruce. Those long-tailed, black-white-and-
green birds flying up from the road are magpies, and that's
a crested jay scolding from the branches. If you draw up
to photograph the doe and her fawn at the wood's edge,
you can know by their big ears that they are mule deer.
And you may even see an unkempt dog slinking off into
the tall timber, and realize that he is that blood brother of
loneliness, the coyote.

Later or sooner, you will discover Aspen, a town become
world-famous, to the surprise of its 1,500 citizens, remnant
of the 15,000 whose hearts beat high in bonanza times.
When the silver boom closed with the last century, Aspen,

isolated in its cup of mountains, was forgotten. But it was those steep slopes and the perfect snows upon them which brought it to life again in the thirties. Now it is a sports resort known to skiers internationally, with the longest of all chair lifts, and runs that brought to it in 1950 a contest for the ski championships of the world. In summer quite the other way; brain replaces brawn. In the forties, sparked by eastern know-how and money, enthusiasm for Aspen caught fire again, and yearly burns high in a cultural festival. Visitors flock to attend lectures, concerts, forums, and seminars, sitting at the feet of renowned artists and thinkers. All this has made of little old Aspen a flavorous mixture of Old West and slaloms, of high thinking and good living. People of note elect to live for a while in the Victorian mansions next the new Swiss chalets, and the hotel, dating from the plush eighties, keeps its early charms with its new comforts.

While winter and summer are Aspen's big season, I'd choose to be there in autumn; indeed, that goes for all Colorado. For one thing, in the last half of September and first of October the flashing stream of highway traffic has dwindled and a night's lodging is easily found. But what brings me to the Rockies then is Aspen's own tree, the trembling aspen, which sends to glory all the mountainsides. Turning from pale summer green to gold molten with sunlight, the white-stemmed aspens stand like angels against the naked blue of the fall sky. They pour down the slopes in sheets of fire colors, and troop, brilliant and whispering, through the somber masses of silent spruce and fir. Small wonder that the Denver and Rio Grande runs special night trains from Denver to Steamboat Springs, where pilgrims go by motor on day-long "aspencades."

From Aspen, or anywhere else, to Mesa Verde National Park, 'way down in the southwest corner of Colorado, is a long pull. And a strong one, if you come over the giddy twists and grades of the Million Dollar Highway through Ouray and Silverton. You'll be journeying not only miles into lonely splendor, but centuries back in time. "Mesa Verde," of course, means "green table," and that precisely describes this lofty plateau which rises out of the burning desert, covered with a low, aromatic forest of juniper and pinyon pine and carved with deep, steep canyons. And in the niches of these walls you'll stare to see the silent, ancient habitations of the Indian cliff dwellers. There are hundreds of such ruins in Mesa Verde, and in them archaeologists have found relics which you may wonder at in the museum there—seeds stored by these first American farmers, cloth their women wove, weapons of the hunt, baskets and pottery—even doll dishes shaped by the fingers of little girls "helping mother." Now they are gone, those people who loved the things you are loving—this desert sun and air, the scent of juniper, the far croak of the ravens sailing over the chasm—gone two hundred years before Columbus ever came upon America.

From Mesa Verde you may want to swing around through New Mexico to visit the swarming pueblos of today. Taos in particular is the mecca of all who specialize in the art, folklore, and religion of Southwest Indian life. From there you can drop down to Santa Fe, where the historic Spanish flavor is cherished by a colony of painters and writers. Or you can cut through the mountains to the tourist center of Colorado Springs, nestled at the foot of Pike's Peak. The mountain's discoverer, young Zebulon, predicted that its awesome height could never be conquered, but now a paved road and a cog railway run right to the summit. Next favorite excursion is to the Garden of the Gods, that fantastic wilderness of strangely shaped, great red rocks amid gnarled junipers older than Methuselah. Go early, before the bumper-to-bumper defile begins, when the young day is fresh and nobody is there but the gods and you. You, and high in bright morning, the wheeling swifts and the white-crested giant Pike.

Through the passes of the Rockies, just yesterday, journeyed the pioneering heroes of our Homeric age—Lewis and Clark, Marcus and Narcissa Whitman, Kit Carson and Jim Bridger. In all our struggle to conquer a continent, it was the Rockies, above all, that tried and proved the American will. And even in our day, when those perils are past, this range, the very backbone of our country, makes any man who comes to it stand tall and breathe deep with native pride.

The Canyon and the Dam

Now *here are paired phenomena that are emphatically American. The Grand Canyon of the Colorado River is famous all over the world as one of its seven wonders. About the other six there might be argument, with claims raised for this cataract, that volcano, or pyramid, or cathedral. (The mighty ruins of Angkor usually get on the list, and you who have seen them must tell me, when we meet again, how high to place them there.) But the Grand Canyon would be one of everybody's seven, and probably first in most counts. For it is acknowledged, even by those who have never seen it, to be unsurpassed in vastness, antiquity, and splendor. Indeed, the National Park Rangers stationed there say that the foreigners who visit it are better informed and more eager about it than our people, for in their own lands they have long read and thought of it as the most representative thing in all our country.*

I wish it were. And perhaps it is. Perhaps we do well to elect to represent us the thing which lifts our spirits to their noblest heights. Of course, among the awed and silenced, there are always the wisecrackers also. "What a hell of a place to lose a cow!" But that's American, too, the laugh at anything, good or bad, that is a bit too much for us.

Those who "take in" the Canyon (which can't be done, in fact) nowadays also visit the dam. And Boulder Dam, or Hoover Dam as it has been superfluously re-entitled, is magnificently ours, the grandest example of American know-how that one could wish to see. But what one sees, despite its monumental beauty, is to my mind only the concrete part of that know-how.

For the dam, a federal project, is built by all of us, all of us taxpayers. It is directly for the benefit of only part of us, but we have all been proud to have a hand in it. We know, in masonry like this, how to employ the powers deriving from the consent of the governed. These powers which bridled this bucking broncho of all western rivers, must now cope with forces far more violent. They will be able to only if our consent is granted with great care and wisdom.

THERE is a giant who once claimed dominion over one-thirteenth of the area of this country—the Colorado River. It had a score of other young giants, only comparatively smaller, working for it in six great states. All together they used to carry away to the sea about seven-

teen million cubic yards of American soil every year. Their
united strength is five million prime horsepower. Kicking
horsepower, rearing, bucking, locoed horsepower it was,
before puny man threw a halter over it.

The Colorado was born the wickedest stream in the world.
For a thousand miles, flowing far, far below the surface of
the surrounding country, it gouged away the land, so that
though your life might depend on getting one handful of
its muddy waters to drink, you could wander till you
dropped before you could find a way down its sheer sides.
Yet it has repeatedly gone berserk in flood. From its beginning it was a boom-and-bust river. After running low along
its bed of gigantic rocks it might in a single night—after
heavy rains or sudden melting of the snows—rise to a tide
that could destroy everything in its path. Emerging from
the prison corridor of its wall, this torrent devastated vast
areas in California and Arizona, every year building higher
the barren, queasy delta at its mouth, and lashing restlessly
over this wasteland till it spent its rage in the Gulf of
California.

Seventeen hundred miles from that muddy mouth, rises
the pure source of the Colorado. This headstream, called
the Green, is the high-born child of the Wind River
Mountains in Wyoming. At their breasts of snow the little
Green is nursed, and runs laughing away, down through
forests of lodgepole pines, till it reaches the sagebrush
plains. There it slips stealthily, with no hint of the fury
to come, between its waterweeds and swallow-haunted
banks, until it must break through Utah's mountains.
Then for the next thousand miles the whole course of the

river is a commingling of horror and beauty. And in that course, through the long ages, the Colorado has carved the greatest of all natural masterpieces—the Grand Canyon.

As you stand on the Canyon's brink, your speechless wonder is but an echo of the eternal silence welling from below, and the river, distantly glinting like a silver thread, seems the least of the spectacle. Yet the river itself carved that gulf ten miles wide, a mile deep, and 217 miles long. Its tributaries are the architects of those crumbling temples of red and gold, the sculptors of those unfinished images of gods so old that even as you watch them they melt into the purple shadows.

And here the Colorado has laid open the book of life, so that modern man may read the story from a great stone page. Millions of years of earth's history are represented by the slow accumulation of these rocks that once were sediments of seas and lakes which came and went many times. The river, which in its effort to cut through the rocks as the plateau was uplifted, has cut down, down through the Permian limestones and sandstones that accumulated 215 million years ago, laying bare the fossil tracks of prehistoric reptiles that once walked here as confidently as tourists do today. Down, down through the great "Red Wall" of Mississippian limestone (now 300 million years old) the river has rasped, unearthing, in the layers above, fossils of ferns. Today it is filing away furiously at the hard black schists and pink granites of the Archaean Era, a mile below the canyon rim—rocks so old that they antedate the appearance of life on earth.

Time, in this shining void, is nothing, and man's first few

thousand years on this planet appear, truly, as the last tick of the clock. A million years from now men may still stand at the head of the Bright Angel Trail and gaze in awe like yours and mine at a Canyon grown grander. Or if there should be no men then, as there are no dinosaurs now, the same wind of the world will blow here, whispering to the ear of the pines remembrance of elemental things, and prophesying more to come.

The first white man who ever saw America's grandest sight was Don Lopez de Cardenas, one of Coronado's lieutenants who, in 1540, with twelve other conquistadores, abruptly found himself on the South Rim, gazing in speechless astonishment. His men attempted to descend but soon crawled back from the brink. For cliffs that seem no higher than a man were found to be "taller than the great tower of Seville." How many times taller even the Don could not grasp, for the scale of the Canyon is so vast that it dawns only slowly, and even today the visitor can hardly believe that the Empire State Building could be tucked out of sight beneath one of the Canyon's many cliffs.

For more than two hundred years after Cardenas, the Canyon was not seen again by any white man, and not till 1826 did an American, James O. Pattie, the great pioneer, behold it. He and his son became the first white men ever to follow up the Canyon as they trapped for beaver. Its depths remained unscaled, its river uncharted, though as the famous scouts and trappers of the West pushed ever farther, one after another tried to force his way down the forbidding current, only to be driven back. Fed by Indian fear of the river, legends about the Colorado multiplied.

Some people claimed it flowed underground for great distances; some reported that its course was interrupted by waterfalls higher than Niagara; fugitive "bad men" were believed to haunt the Canyon as a hideout, and bands of fierce Utes certainly roamed the rim. Time flowed by, while Arizona became American territory, and gold was discovered in California, the Civil War was fought, the continent linked by rails, and still the Colorado, throughout much of its course, remained unmapped, unknown, the most mysterious and terrifying river in the world.

Then on a May day in 1869, at the town of Green River, Wyoming, while coolies and cowboys and railroad men and Indians watched, a band of nine men put four boats into the Green's flood. Their leader, Major John Wesley Powell, was determined to lick the Colorado with one hand. He had lost his right arm at Shiloh. Schoolteacher, botanist, geologist, surveyor, this thirty-five-year-old Illinois veteran, more scholar than explorer, had worked for two years on his plans and wrung from Congress and the Smithsonian Institute a small fund for traveling expenses. His men, young but toughened to western life, were to receive $75 apiece, when they emerged from the jaws of death; the Major himself drew no salary. And the trip was no "stunt" like going over Niagara Falls in a barrel. Powell was out to map and master the most unbridled of all rivers, to explore the Canyon's billion years of geology.

His twenty-one-foot boats were of stout oak, with air chambers to right them in case of capsizing. Without their cargoes they could be portaged by four men. The equipment of repair materials and tools, food for ten months, clothing, firearms, and scientific instruments loaded the boats deeply, as they sped down Flaming Gorge. It was in Ladore Canyon, at Disaster Falls that the first of their boats was smashed to bits. Into Whirlpool Canyon spun the three remaining craft, with one man already deserting, and on through Desolation Canyon and the endless Labyrinth. In and out of water all day, never dry, their food already moldering, the boats water-logged from loss of paint, the little band pushed on through Cataract Canyon, past Dirty Devil Creek, under the shadow of the Orange Cliffs that Powell climbed to sight the Unknown Mountains.

Day after day, driving himself relentlessly, the one-armed Major toiled with his instruments up perilous walls to take observations and map his course. Strong young men though they were, his companions were exhausted after the run through Sockdologer Rapids. Lowering boats on ropes, portaging them for miles over rocks, often making but three miles a day, by dint of superhuman effort, they had forced their way through Marble Canyon and were now in the depths of the Grand Canyon's granites. With nerves frayed, they broke into quarrels; waves, rocks, and rapids no worse than those they had surmounted, looked, after the strain of the Sockdologer, appalling. Indeed, every Canyon explorer who lived to tell the tale, speaks of a strange river fear that is peculiar to the Colorado. Not the bravest man but has known it to overpower him, sometimes quite unexpectedly and after weeks of surmounting every obstacle.

In such a mood, perhaps, three of the Powell party, on August 28, either refused to continue the journey, or, as some say, were finally driven from the expedition by the overstrained Major. The truth of the dissension can never now be known. After taking their share of the rations and a duplicate set of the Major's records, in case he should perish, they climbed up out of the Canyon. Three days later Powell's party emerged from the Grand Canyon to find white men, at the anxious request of the Government, scanning the water for their corpses or any fragment of their wreckage. At that point the Major left the river, since it had been explored from there to its mouth many times. But the three who had quit were never seen again. Later it was discovered that Indians had killed them almost as soon as they reached the rim.

And only then did Powell discover that in the emotional tension at "Separation Rapids" he had given the other party not only a duplicate set of his records, but the original too, of a large segment of his journey. So two years later Powell ran through his whole course again, without the loss of a single man, and with the most complete scientific records resulting. Thereafter Powell was soon made chief of the new United States Geological Survey, and became its greatest organizer, giving it the imprint that makes of it still a model government service.

But exploring the Colorado wasn't conquering it. Not long after Powell's second trip, it drowned the president of the Denver and Rio Grande Railroad, with two companions, while he was surveying it with the romantic idea of building a railway through it. Against many successful trips through the Colorado canyons must be reckoned tragedies; some of the skeletons found beside the river have never been identified. One rash couple essayed a honeymoon trip down the river and perished together. As late as 1929, Glen Sturdevant, naturalist of Grand Canyon National Park, and Ranger Fred Johnson lost their lives in the Canyon in line of duty.

The Colorado had bigger game to hunt, too. In 1905 it charged through a levee along its lower banks that had cost California a million dollars to build, rushed down its own irrigation canals, and burst into the below-sea-level Imperial Valley, driving thousands from their homes, ruining farms, washing out communication lines, and vomiting forth the Salton Sea, a lake without an outlet which still submerges 445 square miles.

History and geology show that many times the Colorado has overwhelmed the Imperial Valley. But California could not afford to abandon it to the river. You can raise seven crops of alfalfa a year down there; with its warm winter climate the Valley produces summer vegetables and fruits even in January. All that is needed for fertility is water, the water of the Colorado rushing, useless, to the sea. Beyond the mountains, along the coast of southern California, the fast-growing cities were panting for water too; and they needed light and power, that five million horsepower that was still hitched up to nothing and could still, like wild horses, trample upon one hundred thousand people.

That is why, in 1918, Arthur P. Davis, chief engineer of the Reclamation Service of the Department of Interior, conceived of a dam in Boulder Canyon to conquer the mad flood. It took eleven years of battles in Congress, of complex legal adjustments involving the rights of seven states and Mexico, before the Boulder Dam project became effective by law in June 1929.

Then, only four months later, came the big stock-market crash. As it developed into nation-wide unemployment, Uncle Sam decided to rush the plans for the dam with a nine million dollar annual pay roll. So the most titanic blueprinting job ever laid out by engineers was speeded up with day and night shifts; it was completed six months ahead of schedule. Then the Government threw open the bidding to the contractors. Six Companies, Inc., of San Francisco, won the contract by a bid of $48,890,095.50. This was the lowest bid and, at the same time, the biggest sum ever spent on a single engineering project.

There were plenty to howl calamity. The dam would never hold the river, cried these Jeremiahs; the reservoir would immediately fill up with silt. Workers, it was feared, would not consent to live on a desert where the temperature in summer rises to 130° Fahrenheit. The sheer rock walls of the canyon were thought by some too hard to drill. And there might be no market for such hydroelectric power.

But the engineers were undaunted. They built railroads to the dam, and a network of highroads. They spanned the canyon with bridges and tremendous steel cables. They constructed two huge concrete mixing plants and a gravel-screening plant; they put up machine shops and air-compressor plants, and built a steel-rolling plant right on the spot. Power was brought across two hundred miles of deserts to operate machinery.

To house the army of workmen of all sorts the Govern-

ment rushed to completion within one year the town of
Boulder City, seven miles from the dam, on what, twelve
months before, was only desert. Today Boulder City is as
pretty and well regulated a town as you could want, amply
proving that the simplest way to get rid of slums is not to
build any.

Over the new railroad line were hauled 840 miles of pipe
line for the dam, and twenty-one million pounds of valves
and gates. Forty-five million pounds of steel for reinforce-
ment, five million barrels of cement, were brought to Black
Canyon. Altogether 175,000 carloads of materials were
rushed into the fight with the demoniac river. Nor had anyone ever seen such a massing of strategic weapons. The
gravel-screening plants could wash the raw materials and
place them ready for mixture with cement and water at
the rate of more than 16½ tons a minute. Portable X-ray
machines of 300,000 volts searched the rolled steel plates
for hidden flaws. The air-compression plants built near the
river's edge had a capacity of 14,500 cubic feet a minute.
Thousands of fifty-ton trucks stood ready for the opening
gun of the great battle.

It came with a roar of dynamite as the engineers drove
four tremendous tunnels, two on each side of the canyon,
through which to divert the river through the solid rock.
These were drilled and blasted, alternately, while power
shovels moved away the debris, and trucks carted it off.
The engineers were often working on all four tunnels from
each end at once, making eight spearheads of attack. Fifty-
six feet high—as tall as a four-story building—the four
diversion tunnels were driven at the rate of 256 feet in

twenty-four hours, and over a mile in one month. When three and a half million pounds of dynamite had been used, the tunnels were finished and ready for the Colorado to flow through them.

Now to make it do so! Piles driven out into the river were spanned by a trestle. On this trucks ran out, and dumped their loads of large and small rocks. Within twenty-four hours a coffer dam or dike was formed, forcing the river out of its bed of a million years and sending it seething through the diversion tunnels. Meantime, just above their outlet, a similar dam was built to prevent the river from backing up. Between the two temporary dams the bed of the river was dried by great suction pumps. This was where the great dam was to rise.

Now the "high scalers" went to work. Swung in safety belts on cables over the awful gorge, at the risk (and sometimes the cost) of their lives, they attacked the rock with their drills, smoothing it till they had removed almost a million cubic yards. Then, braced in an arc between the eternal walls, Boulder Dam itself began to rise. The first bucket of cement was poured June 6, 1933; within six months a million cubic yards were in place. Block by block the structure rose, in staggered tiers. Two city blocks thick at base where the most terrible pressure of the water would come, and broad enough at the top for a four-lane auto highway, Boulder Dam rears up 726 feet high, which is a third again as high as the Washington Monument. Engineers' Gothic, it hás a look of airy grace, like a flying buttress, that utterly belies its gigantic strength and weight. Heavier than the Great Pyramid of Egypt, which was twenty years a-building by 100,000 slaves, Boulder Dam was completed in twenty-one months by the labor of 1,200 free men, and the whole project, allotted seven years by contract, was completed two years ahead of schedule.

In the ordinary course, the vast bulk of the dam would have required more than a hundred years for the concrete to cool, and, shrinking as it cooled, it would have cracked. But the engineers had built their dam in separate blocks honeycombed with steel pipes. Ice-cold water was poured through these, and each block separately and swiftly chilled, and then fixed immovably to the next block by flooding the joint with liquid or grout cement. So the dam was already cooled on the day it was finished and stood there flawless, the greatest monolith or solid structure in the world.

And now at last steel gates closed the diversion tunnels. The thwarted river began to rise behind the dam, backing up to make the biggest artificial body of water known— Lake Mead. This lake in the midst of a flaming desert, coolly reflecting the barren red and purple peaks about it, has a five-hundred-mile shore line. Into its depths the river, deprived of all current, is forced to drop harmlessly its tremendous load of mud, before it emerges from valves beneath the dam, in a roiling, emerald swirl, as if the demoniac stream were angry at having to cleanse itself and work for man.

For before the Colorado is allowed to proceed, it is forced to pass through the intake towers that conduct it into the heart of the dam structure, where it must set in motion the hydroelectric works. Each one of the generators —thirteen of the projected seventeen have already been put in place—is the size of a small apartment building, able to create all the electric energy that a metropolis could use, and to bring cheap light to a million customers, and cheap power to the rich mineral deposits scattered over the desert. The output of Boulder Dam—(they call it Hoover Dam these days, but I don't!)—has reached six billion kilowatt-hours a year. It is the sale of this power, transmitted over eleven great power lines looped from steel tower to tower, that is paying off the cost of the dam, bringing in to the Treasury of the United States more than $5,000,000 annually. Our children will see the entire cost of the investment recovered, and from then on it is a gilt-edged income for the taxpayers.

But Uncle Sam isn't through with the Colorado yet. Below Boulder, the Parker Dam is stretched, built with funds supplied by the Metropolitan Water District of Southern California. From Lake Havasu, created by the dam, the pure, unmuddied waters are led away across the Mojave desert, in the longest aqueduct in the world. It crosses waterless valleys and for ninety-two miles it burrows in tunnels under mountain ranges, to bring clear drinking water to the multimillion population of Los Angeles and her satellites. Still lower down, the Imperial Dam diverts irrigation water to the Imperial Valley of California and the Gila desert of Arizona through long canals streaking across the Martian landscape of the southwest. And yet more dams, on the Colorado's tributaries, are under way.

Wherever a dam is built, the river's magician fingers are made to touch the soil, and truck farms spring up. Where once was only creosote bush or sagebrush, long-staple cotton can be grown, or sugar beets. Light, almost as cheap as water, flashes on in mining towns that huddled in darkness once under the arid peaks, and through the new, cheap power the wealth of the southwestern states in manganese, silver, copper, lead, zinc, molybdenum, vanadium, and uranium can be exploited now. May God, who wrought the Canyon, guide man to use with wisdom the potentials that he has unlocked by Boulder Dam!

The Mother Lode—
Cradle of California

❧

The searches for the Golden Fleece, for the Golden Apples of the Hesperides, are legends of classic beauty. They suit the weary dignity of countries where the study of Greek is part of a gentleman's education. Here in this far western state we have a story of our own about the hunt for gold, and it's all true, and not a bit gentlemanly. But I think the epic of the Gold Rush will endure as long as any.

The foothills where it happened, however, seem scarcely to remember it any more, so drowsily empty are they now, in the thin shade of "digger" pines and the sunshine of spring, when the wildflowers dance over the slopes—tidy-tips and gilia, cats'-ears and owl's clover. With summer the dream deepens there, and the still heat grows. So you must have found it, with Alice, when you slipped away there for a few days between your wedding and the summons to Washington for training. I know June in those Sierra foot-hills, fragrant with drying grasses, threaded with the chitin-

ous monotony of insect notes. I can guess how, amid the humid, crowded scenes of tropical Asia, you must remember, almost wondering, that sere and sweetly lonely place where—if ever a young man did—you struck it rich.

G OLD and love affairs are hard to hide," says a Spanish proverb. Yet the vein so rich it is known as the Mother Lode, amassed through the ages by the wild streams washing it down from California's Sierra Nevada, remained a glittering secret until exactly 7:30 A.M. on the twenty-fourth of January, 1848.

At that moment, at a spot called by the Indians Coloma, on the south fork of the American River, one James Marshall, who was building a lumber and grist mill for the Swiss pioneer, Johann Sutter, walked down to close the millrace. Instead, he let open the floodgates of history.

For there, under six inches of icy clear water, lay a yellow deposit that had not been there the day before. All that glisters is not gold, and Marshall knew about fool's gold (copper or iron pyrites) which fractures when you strike it. But true gold is so malleable that a single ounce of it has been hammered into a leaf 300 feet square; it is so ductile that one gram can be drawn out into a wire two miles long. With a rock Marshall pounded at these yellow nuggets from the stream. They didn't fracture. They flattened out and out.

Johann Sutter was astounded when his mill foreman burst in on him late of a rainy winter afternoon at Sutter's Fort (now part of the city of Sacramento, then an outpost in the wilderness). But when Marshall had untied the rag he carried, Sutter the self-educated businessman dragged open the *Encyclopedia Americana* and found the tests for gold. The first was the acid test; nitric acid will tarnish many metals, but not gold. Sutter had some, and poured it on Marshall's specimens. They did not tarnish. Next he put them to the balance test. Gold outweighs silver, the next heaviest metal. Carefully on his scales the Swiss measured out, in equal volume, some silver and some of the find from the American River. Inexorably, the gold sank.

The two men stared, awed, at the future, and then swore each other to secrecy. But Marshall had already talked, and Sutter was no more discreet, so by March of 1848 the secret was out and spreading. And just as Sutter feared, the results were disastrous for him. In the wild stampede for gold, squatters stole his lands and lumber, ruffians the goods off the shelves of his store; his farm hands left the harvest to rot, his clerks and servants quit the Fort. All over California, ranches were thus abandoned, shops were closed, soldiers deserted from Army posts, and the detachments sent out to capture them deserted too. As ships came into San Francisco, crews and officers alike took off for the gold fields.

Blacksmiths left their anvils, bakers their loaves, and editors printed the news of the wild scramble only as long as they could stand it—one truant editor, with only pick, shovel, and pan, averaged takings of $100 a day.

For in those first months everybody had luck. The nuggets were right there in the stream beds, and under the tree stumps. No wonder that one miner extracted six ounces of gold from holes in a rock, as easily, he said, as pulling the kernels from hickory nuts. Another gathered two and a half pounds of gold in fifteen minutes. A trench one hundred feet long and a few feet wide yielded to two men $17,000 in a week. Takings of $8000 in a day were claimed.

When easy pickings were panned out in one place, these Forty-Eighters moved lightheartedly on, along the Lode that runs 277 crooked miles through the foothills. Thus all the gold-bearing streams of the Sierra Nevada were superficially explored very early—the Feather and American rivers, the rivers with Indian names like Yuba, Tuolumne, Consumnes, Mokelumne, and the Spanish-sounding Calaveras and Merced. Soon these names would ring around the world, stock companies be founded on their auriferous sands. For an estimated $10,000,000 in gold was produced from the Mother Lode in the last seven months of 1848.

But so slow was communication between California and the Atlantic seaboard that not until September did the first news of the gold strike peep out of a few lines of type in the Baltimore *Sun*. Many people regarded the tale as a hoax—until a twenty-four-pound nugget of California gold was officially assayed by the United States Mint and put on display in Washington and New York.

It was then too late in the season to cross the snowbound Rockies, so the first Argonauts crowded a sailing vessel that left New York in October; by January of 1849, ninety vessels had cleared eastern ports. Some made the long costly voyage around the Horn. Others sailed to Panama where the adventurers crossed the Isthmus and then went aboard another craft bound for San Francisco. Some impatient gold-seekers even tried to paddle log canoes from Panama to San Francisco. So crowded were many ships that scurvy and cholera made of them floating pesthouses. Yellow fever and malaria lurked along the Panama route. Unseaworthy vessels, pressed into service and jammed with fortune hunters, disappeared without a trace. Yet in the first month alone of that illustrious year of '49, eight thousand eager Argonauts passed through the Golden Gate.

With the coming of spring the overland rush began. It took many routes, some as far south as Mexico, others as far north as Oregon, but all fraught with hardships for which the tenderfeet were ill-prepared. Some set out on foot expecting to push wheelbarrows all the way to California, some came in prairie schooners with women and children— pathetic hostages to fortune. The sudden influx of thousands of white men, all armed, aroused Comanches, Sioux, Apaches, Cheyennes, Yumas, and Utes. Mountains and deserts were strewn with scalped corpses, burned wagons, dead animals, leathern trunks, abandoned utensils. Often the Indians had no need to attack; instead from hiding they watched axles break, mules and oxen die, men drink poisonous water. Several wagon trains blundered into Death Valley, others became snowbound in the Sierra Nevada. At one time twenty thousand men, women and children were waiting, desperate and helpless, east of the Sierra. To their rescue went men like Major Rucker of the U.S. Army, and William Waldo of the generous Sacramento Relief Committee. Let us hope their treasure is laid up in heaven.

The average Forty-Niner was in his twenties. Many were well born and well educated—except in mining; they seldom thought of bringing a shovel and, once arrived, had to pay $100 for one. Yet these young men, within a year, had begun to work out for themselves, on principles of fair play and common sense, the mining laws that became models in the later gold strikes in Australia, the Transvaal, Paraguay, and are still influential in American mining law today.

And such was the comradeship in that first era of good feeling that a pick and shovel left on the stream bank were enough to establish a claim. Newcomers were welcomed, and shown how to build a rocker or cradle for sifting the gold from the stream. Compassion was common; when a lad of sixteen arrived hungry and penniless, a bunch of miners panned all day to grubstake him. Single women were so scarce they could wed upon arrival. One seventeen-year-old boy rode thirty-five miles merely to look at a lady "just like Mother." A little girl was adored as queen of the camp. Tents, shacks, curtains of muslin stretched over bush-tops were all that most Forty-Niners had to shelter them. Sundays were devoted to bathing, writing home, spreading washing on the banks. If you could find a Mexican woman to do your wash it cost $20 for eight pieces; some miners mailed their washing to Canton, China—as cheaper and better done! A potato or a candle sold for $1, sugar for $3 a pound, sardines at $4 a can, flour up to $800 a barrel. Yet so ready was the "dust" to pay that luxuries sometimes came to camp before many of the necessities, and even champagne and oysters were presently available to the man who struck it rich. When that happened, he celebrated with a spree for the whole camp, and might risk the rest of his gains at the gambling tables. If he lost the lot he went cheerfully back to cooking his own beans and biscuit, confident that the Mother Lode was boundless in her generosity.

But 1850 saw a change in the numbers and kind of the gold-seekers. The wildfire news had run to the ends of the earth; in far corners men tossed at night dreaming of fortune for the taking. For this was free gold, on land in the public domain, belonging to him who claimed it. Never before in civilized times had wilderness thus offered treasure to any, citizen or not, with no overlord to demand a share. So this, the first international gold rush in history, brought to our western shore hard-working Germans, Frenchmen courteous and clannish; stocky, superstitious Cornish miners, men equally experienced from Mexico, Peru, and Chile, "Kanakas" from the remote Marquesas Islands, tough Australians, and silent, pigtailed Chinese in droves. Some Argonauts imported gangs of Hawaiians; southerners brought their slaves only to find that these Negroes were free, by law, as soon as they touched Californian soil, and others hired the local Indians to do their digging for them.

These motley hordes crowded along the Lode in swift-

springing towns named with crude American poetry—
Squabbletown, Fiddletown, Rough and Ready, Poker Flat,
Slumgullion, Hoodoo Bar. Or they bore melodious Spanish
syllables—Mariposa, Melones, wild Hornitos of fifteen
thousand souls. Any one of them might boast three dozen
saloons, for this was a man's world still; at the boisterous
dances a white armband proclaimed that one of the booted
partners was a lady. The real women in their lives were, for
the most, a continent and more away, and tedium was as
wearing as hardship. No wonder they baited bull against
grizzly bear, or flocked to the Mexican gambling halls for
faro and monte. The fandango became a favorite of men
from Maine and Ohio and Georgia, and the Spanish
dancing girl took her ounce of gold (about $18) from
Norte Americano as readily as from compatriots.

But for the red-shirted miner the gold came harder now.
As the surface diggings were worked out, men turned to
the "dry placers"—the gravels of long extinct rivers whose
beds had been lifted with the rising of the Sierra. A scramble
up the mountainside began; the earth was torn up,
heaped into sifted tailings, dug in long troughs, piled in
mounds like the waves of a frozen sea. Hydraulic mining
was tried next; water was brought from the Sierra streams in
long flumes, crossing valleys on aqueducts, passing under
mountains by tunnels, to be shot from giant nozzles. Thus
whole hillsides were torn down by water under heavy pressure,
and the gravels and quartz ores made to yield up their
gold.

It was the miners of Spanish strain who best understood
how to get gold out of quartz ore. They introduced the

arrastra, a crushing mill operated by mule- or water-power, which reduced the ore to fragments. These were treated with mercury, which forms an amalgam with gold; the quartz could then be washed free of these heavy metals, and next the mercury was driven off by high temperatures, leaving the gold pure. Thus the Latin Americans did too well to please the Yankees; attempts to oust them brought armed clashes.

For at the Midas touch of the yellow metal, anger and greed in the swarming camps began to harden into crime. Men stole from each other's rockers by night; they formed armed gangs to drive the lone prospector from his claim, or forced him by torture to show where he hid his findings. The stagecoaches carrying away the gold were held up and robbed. Card-sharpers and whisky-sellers became the leeches of the camps, and "Centipede Sal" and her unlovely kind appeared out of their underworld. Duels, brawls, robbery with murder took about 4,200 lives on the Lode between 1848 and 1854. Mokolumne Hill had a killing a week for seventeen weeks. Nobody cared too much if one bad man wiped out another, but when an innocent man was the victim, the citizenry enforced its own justice in a "necktie party" from the bough of the nearest oak; thus did the towns of First Garrote and Second Garrote get their grim names.

All this time the Chinese had been quietly penetrating the Mother Lode country. By 1854, forty-five thousand had come to Kum Shan, "the Golden Hills," as they called California. They were mostly coolies in blue shirts and baggy trousers and wide conical bamboo hats, their worldly goods in a bundle at each end of a pole across the shoulders. Later came merchants in flowered silks, then opium-den proprietors, gamblers, and a pitiful drove of some sixteen thousand slave girls. They brought, too, their gods, and for them built their joss houses or temples, so that the incense of punk sticks strangely tinged the clear western air.

Where others had cleaned out the diggings, the Chinese came to glean—and took out fortunes! In one instance, they asked only to be allowed to occupy a row of deserted shacks; secretly tunneling beneath their floors, they brought up unguessed wealth. At Moore's Flat, two poor coolies on an abandoned placer discovered a $30,000 nugget; knowing it would be claimed by the land's former owners, they chipped it into "dust." Thus did the "heathen Chinese" get his reputation of deceitful devil. Pacific, unarmed, thrifty, he tempted the brutality of others, chief among them the brigand Joaquin Murietta. When the governor of California offered $1000 reward for Murietta's capture, the Chinese raised the ante by $3000, and when at last the bandit was cornered and shot, Chinese Camp went on a firecracker spree of rejoicing.

By 1853 the Mother Lode had reached the peak of its production—$7,613,487 in gold for that single year. But individual placer miners were often making no more than a dollar a day. Placer mining was through; the remaining gold lay deep in the earth, in quartz ore. That meant the sinking of shafts, tunnels through solid rock, stamping mills. At Grass Valley, the workings of the Empire-Star ran over two hundred miles under earth, and plunged a mile deep. The total production of those mines alone had passed $120,000,000. The Big Bonanza at Sonora in 1870 had a peak week when it paid half a million dollars, and a single day in which it reached a production of $160,000 between sunrise and sunset. It is worked to this day.

But such mines require great capital investment, which means the formation of stock companies, often distant. Of those who profit thereby, only a few, like George Hearst, the father of the late famed newspaper man, wielded pick and pan, changed with the changing techniques, steered their way through the intricacies of high finance, and successfully reinvested in greater mine holdings. More commonly, miners sold out at some favorable moment. Thus Leland Stanford cashed in at nearly half a million dollars, put his money into the Central Pacific (ultimately the Union Pacific), and so became a railway magnate and founder of a great university. His friend Mark Hopkins started out as a simple gulch miner, sleeping on his boots for pillow, cooking his "sowbelly" right beside his rocker. With his first success he went to Sacramento, bought a wagonload of needed hardware, sold it in Hangtown for big profit, and so built up a huge business. Philip D. Armour opened a small butcher shop for meat-hungry miners, and thus founded the Chicago packing firm.

Then there was "Wheelbarrow John," who failed to find gold. Back in South Bend, Indiana, he had been a wheelwright. So he began building wheelbarrows for luckier Argonauts; soon he couldn't fill the orders that came his way. When placer mining petered out, and wheelbarrows gave way to mine shafts, John went home; he was next heard from as a wagon builder for Uncle Sam in the Civil

War. In 1912 he revisited Placerville as an automobile magnate. The citizens turned out with a band to welcome him, and a banner that read: *"Welcome, John Studebaker, Gold is where YOU found it."*

In a cabin on Jackass Hill, one man struck the golden vein of humor that first glinted in "The Jumping Frog of Calaveras County" and went on to make the name of Mark Twain immortal. Bret Harte spent only a few months on the Lode, probably as an expressman, but with his short stories mined the ore of its romantic legends for the rest of his life.

It is now a century past, that Homeric age of our Far West, and what is left is a lovely ghost well worth a pilgrimage. State Highway 49 follows the Mother Lode along epic rivers, among tranquil hills where the once ravaged earth still shows weals beneath its grass and dancing mariposa lilies. And here are the Gold Rush towns, or what is left of them—sometimes a village drowsy and content with the ebb of its once flooding life, sometimes no more than a crumbling adobe wall, a jail door swinging in the wind, with fool's oats growing in what was a street.

Coloma has become a state park, its few remaining buildings smothered in roses, perhaps the same tended by James Marshall who passed his last days here as a humble gardener. Another ward of the state is Columbia, the town most triumphantly surviving, since it was built of brick, with fine old ironwork. The park system is working out a complete and authentic restoration here—saloons, hotel, Wells Fargo office, even the gaudy fire engines with their buffalo-hide hose. Along these dreaming streets the trees of heaven mingle their shade with the sweet locusts that came with the women folk from back East.

For, once the easy pickings were taken, "Centipede Sal" decamped, and "Oh, Susannah," who had waited and cried so long, came at last with needle and skillet, with her china tea set, slips of her home roses, her church membership, her deep-hearted family purpose. So the adventurer of yesterday turned to ranching, business, the professions. California was born with a golden spoon in its mouth. But it was cradled in the rockers of the Forty-Niners, and there, out of a moiling current, was panned its true metal.

The Spark on the Anvil

Wherever the living is hard, and men must struggle on with it, lonely and sore and homesick, there may come to them a visitation of those light-winged, gallant folk, the entertainers. What weight they have in the balance against despair, those blithe performances! From New Guinea to the Aleutians, that was proved in the last great war, and in Korea too.

Such programs today, sponsored by USIA throughout Southeast Asia, have us at home laughing and blinking at their success. "Here in Phnom Penh," says one of your earlier letters, "we are swamped with our preparations for our impending 'American Cultural Festival,' which is to open with the arrival of a gifted Onondaga, one 'Tom Two Arrows,' who will do tribal dances, and literally whoop it up. What the jolly Khmers will make of him I don't know. As soon as he arrives we are sending him up to Kompong Cham, one of our provincial towns which has been making great preparations for him. He is to be carried part way up the river in a pirogue, getting off at the Kompong Cham

*dock where he will be met by two hundred Cambodian
children dressed in American Indian headdress. . . . Then
we will have the Westminster College Choir, followed later
by Benny Goodman and his band, then a harmonica vir-
tuoso, the Harlem Globe-Trotters, and the San Francisco
ballet."*

*Now let me tell you about a tiny trouper who also danced
and laughed her way through hardships to lift the hearts
of men, some hundred years ago.*

◥

G OLD is the standard. We say, "This child was good
as gold all day"; we say, "That man has a heart of
gold."

In a small circle of it, we claim a woman's whole life; in
a locket of it, we frame a cherished face. Such a face,
merry between dark red ringlets, shines out at me from the
wild millrace of the Gold Rush days. In that miraculous
year of forty-nine men tore up the beds of rivers and washed
down the very hills; some found fortune and some found
heartbreak. What I have found in their story, that has the
pure gleam of the best about it, is the mutual love of
Lotta Crabtree and the Forty-Niners.

We call them the Forty-Niners, by a convention, and

conventionally they are represented as bearded old men. The fact is that the first to reach the Mother Lode came in '48 and the bulk of them didn't arrive till the early fifties, when Lotta was a tiny girl. And they were young men, young and brave and lusty; they had to be. They had to have the muscle and the digestion and the hope of young men. Bearded they were, but then so would they have been if they had stayed in college or on the farm; that was the style. Young men wore beards, little girls wore pantalets, and minded their manners, and sat small and quiet —all but Lotta.

There is a road, numbered by the proudly sentimental state of California *Route 49*, that today follows the spent Mother Lode as a finger may trace a vital vein down the flesh. It winds in and around and over the foothills of the Sierra Nevada mountains, the golden hills, bright gold of poppies, tarnished gold of fool's oats. It crosses all the fateful rivers—the American, the Stanislaus, the Feather, the Merced,—those icy streams that fevered men's minds with the gleam and glint in their rapids. It clings dizzily to their gorges, and wanders sleepily under blue oaks and gray pines where in spring the long grass is lighted with the swift-withering foothill flowers—fairy lanterns and Chinese houses, cat's-ears and harvest bells.

I never took a highway that was so much a byway; I never saw so few other cars, or so many ghosts. Five thousand men toiled at once on "Mok Hill," miners' shorthand for the legendary Mokolumne whose core was solid gold, they vowed. Hangtown and Dogtown, Angel's Camp and Cherokee Flat, Volcano and Columbia, and all the remnant mining camps where now the sunbaked boards and bricks doze in the sun, teemed once with men of many races and one lust. At Hornitos there were fifteen thousand Mexicans, and at Melones more. There was French Bar, and Nigger Hill, and Dutchman's Flat; there were Chileans and Bolivians and Australians flocking to grub fortune from the ground, and throughout the camps, in settlements of their own, dwelt some twenty thousand pigtailed Chinese, whose very origin is mysterious, so suddenly did they arrive like bees at a honeypot. They had their joss houses, here in the innocent hills, with paper prayers and smoke of devil-chasing punk; they had their opium dreams, and their market for slave girls with lily feet—here where now only the mariposa lilies step across the grass to the call of the valley quail.

But in the "Northern Diggings," in Grass Valley, lived a community of sensible folk, like your people and mine, Oregonians mostly, who put up churches and schools, and planted slips of rose and box, and held the red clay banks with stone walls built to last. The roses are old now, the maples tall, the town still hale, climbing its hills with sturdy vigor. You'd say there was something of western New England in its old white houses, some rectitude and plain pride. One of them on the main street, the primmest one, is modestly marked "The Home of Lotta Crabtree." And down the street, just a door or two away, a brown house burdened with exuberant vines stands treasuring its legend, fantastically true. Out of that deep doorway, in the day when its paint was fresh, steps into my story a woman of breath-taking and notorious beauty. Her eyes were dark and bold and bright; her mouth gave promises and kept them; her flesh was white and smooth as a fallen magnolia petal. Upon her shoulder perched a cockatoo, snowy white against the night of her hair, and as she sailed up the street into town the women sewing at their windows craned to see, and cried to one another in knowing virtue, "There goes Lola Montez!"

" 'Montez,' indeed! An Irish girl, she was born, out of County Limerick—plain Eliza Gilbert."

"Plain she could never be. And she likes to be called the Countess of Lansfeldt."

"Easy enough, maybe, to be a countess if you're a king's mistress." The beautiful dancer passes from sight and the curtain drops over the pane again.

The children caught the kisses that she blew them, and waved after her. "She has a tame bear," one told another. "She has cages of pretty birds."

"She lets us into her garden; she comes out and plays with us—Blindman's Buff and London Bridge."

"Are you going to her party? She gives away favors."

"Plenty of 'em," in her day, the miners agreed among themselves, with a chuckle of pride in it. For proud they were that Lola, scandalous and fabulous and more than a little absurd, had chosen Grass Valley for rustication— proud of her beauty and even her sins, as the men of Troy were proud of stolen Helen's. Her favors from the mad King Ludwig of Bavaria, her trial for bigamy in London, her tarantella with rubber spiders shaken from her skirts, her horsewhipping of a too forthright editor—all this was spice for the talent she lacked. Not for her dancing does theatrical history make honored place for La Montez, nor yet for her beauty or disrepute. But it was she who led forth into the spotlight the laughing child who came to be forthwith the best-loved entertainer ever produced by the American stage.

"I declare, Mrs. Crabtree, how can you let Lotta run in and out of that house? The things she might learn!"

Mary Ann Crabtree stared her critic down. "Jigs and songs and how to make her bow. Lotta's got a gift for all that. 'Twas the psalmist himself who danced before the Lord, and I'll thank you to leave Lotta's bringing up to me."

For Mary Ann Crabtree, sempstress and daughter of a sempstress, boardinghouse keeper and wife to a ne'er-do-well, hid behind a front as plain as the house she lived in a true genius for show business. Crabtree was no good to her and her child, and never would be. Lotta must make her own way in the world, and that way now led over the grassy hills, under the gray pine and the blue oak; the eight-year-old child astride her quick pony and Montez riding graceful beside her, up into the mountains, to the zone of cedar and fir, to the roaring camp of Rough and Ready.

It is a pause in the winding road today, it is a tiny post office with an oxcart wheel and an American flag set in front of the door, a few faded houses among their old rose bushes and great elms, and one small building, too far gone to stand much longer, that bears the still legible name of Fippen, whose blacksmith shop this was. Within, where only shadows throng, a beam of sunlight slanting through

a crack gleams on the anvil where that day the spark of
fame was struck. For Rough and Ready, rough as any camp
in all the roistering Mother Lode and ready now for any
kind of fun, turned out at the news that Lola was in town.
Into old Fippen's blacksmith shop the miners came crowding, laughing, whistling, craning to see the ruined actress
where she stood in all her beauty, blazing with the drama
of the moment. From behind her skirts she drew a tiny
girl, and lifted her onto the anvil. Then, while Lola clapped
her hands for rhythm, the child sprang into a burst of
dancing brilliant as a shower of sparks struck from that
stage of iron. Her fiery red curls danced with a life of their
own. Her toes scarcely touched the anvil, her black eyes
snapped mischief, and as she tossed off highland fling and
fandango she laughed—what other dancer ever had the
breath to do it?—like a Sierra brook glittering with gold.

They cheered and clapped and cried for more of her.
They fell in love with her on the spot, a headlong love that
was to last their lives out, the purest, gayest sort of love
that ever man felt for woman. For she was only an elfish
promise of womanhood, so innocent and merry that she
held out her heart to them in both hands. Pouring herself
into her miraculously precocious and gifted performance,
she offered them a cup of sparkling delight. And thirstily
they drank it, for they were sick for fun and beauty—sick
of the stubborn earth they wrestled with, sick of the icy
streams where all day long they stooped over pan and
rocker, of their womanless discomfort, their beans and
saleratus bread, their leaky shelters, of each other's gaunt
and bearded faces and the dirty faces of the cards that were

all they had had for amusement when the dark came down. They were homesick to the soul, for these first Argonauts were mothers' sons like your boy and mine, young husbands longing for the women they worked for; they were green-horns, most of them, farm boys and city fellows, and these alien hills a wide, wild continent from home held loneli-ness and bitterness for them. Lotta was sweet antidote. The ripe beauty of the adventuress beside her was a fruit ignored. The sun of Lola Montez, indeed, was soon to set in friendless poverty. But the career of Lotta Crabtree was forged that day in 1855 into permanent fame upon the anvil of Rough and Ready.

Montez had played her role out; she had coached the child in the comic and sentimental songs of the day, and taught her reel and jig and ballet step, but the mite re-quired no more lessons in dancing, so completely did she master the most intricate step in her first few attempts. And when Lola wanted to take Lotta with her on a tour of the Australian stage, shrewd little Mrs. Crabtree, though nearly penniless, refused. She moved with Lotta to Rabbit Creek, following her hapless husband's fortunes, and kept her eye on Lotta. Another eye fell on the child there, one night when she danced—the sharp glance of Dr. Robinson, the theatrical manager, and though he had a daughter of his own to promote, he proposed to Mary Ann that they strike a bargain over Lotta. The door he opened led straight to the San Francisco stage, crowded with the greatest theatrical figures of that lavish day. Yet Mary Ann Crab-tree closed it firmly. Lotta was hers to look after.

That night little Sue Robinson was billed to entertain

the Rabbit Creek miners. But all day long the quick fingers
of the sempstress worked furiously, sewing on a tiny costume that was to become famous—a long-tailed green coat,
knee breeches, and a little green hat. Thus, dressed as an
Irish boy, Lotta, on a rough board stage with candles for
footlights, flung herself into jigs and reels and songs in
Irish brogue. From across the street Sue's audience heard
the salvos of applause that shook the log-cabin walls, and
began to drift over to see the fun. They roared with delight
over Lotta's merriment, but when she changed to a demure
white gown with puffed sleeves and sang pathetic ballads,
quarters, half-dollars and great ringing Mexican dollars
rained at her feet. Gold nuggets followed; and the young
performer fled in terror. Imperturbable Mary Ann Crabtree
swept up the tributes with broom and dustpan. Dr. Robinson and Sue retired in unforgiving defeat.

On into that world of sudden fortune and frontier priva-
tion, of hangings and shootings and soft-hearted sentiment,
danced Lotta. Mary Ann had joined her child's fortunes
with a troupe of barnstormers led by one Mart Taylor, who
beat the drums as the company, mounted on mules with
red, yellow, and blue tassels, rode into each eager camp.
From Mart, Lotta learned endless songs with endless verses
—songs of miners' luck, of home and mother, songs of satire
and songs of a cheerful ribaldry that came with delicious
innocence from her child's lips. Mart taught her soft-shoe
dancing; an old-time Negro minstrel taught her clogs and
breakdowns and how to finger the heart-plucking banjo.

The theater would be some grocery store, some gambling
hell, some smoky saloon; the stage was boards laid over

trestles; old blankets formed the curtain. Of scenery there
was none. The child herself was scenery for these homeless
men to feast their eyes upon. Her bright hair framed a
brighter face; her mouth, as sweet and friendly as it was
finely cut, was tucked in deliciously at the corners, as
though to hold back her gaiety. Her eyes were both dark
and frank, and about her small person there was a dainty
childishness that was to last throughout her career. Youth
and joy with all their audacity ran on to the stage when
Lotta did. She could stand there and do nothing but laugh,
in a voice surprisingly hearty for her years, till a whole camp
was laughing with her. She could sing, with tears in her
voice, "How can I leave thee, how can I from thee part?"
so that the wrench of parting tore at every listener too. For
each lonely miner, weary of brawling men, wearier of camp
women, felt then that Lotta was his own little girl, was
all the innocence and happiness that he had left, and longed
for beyond the fortune he hunted.

No one dreamed of the child's stage fright. Or how, when
the show was over, she would be strapped into her saddle at
midnight, there to sleep as she could on a joggling mule till
daylight. When she woke, it might be to the golden grass
of the foothills, starred in spring with those frail, gay wildflowers, or it might be to banks of snow under the solemn
sequoias. Skirting awful precipices, fording white-fanged
rivers, crowded to the edge of the trail by trains of packmules
bringing out gold, the little troupe rode in silence for fear
of highwaymen. No cluster of cabins was too small for them
to seek out for audience. Port Wine, City of Seventy-Six,
Rich Bar, Coarsegold, all the mushroom settlements of the

Mother Lode laughed and wept with Lotta and threw their hearts and their gold at her feet.

Then, and for many years, her only coach was her mother. Mary Ann Crabtree had a genius for timing a laugh, and before she sent her daughter onto the stage, she spent an hour telling jokes and making up ridiculous songs which started the child's inner fountain to spontaneous bubbling. Always friendly to the troupe, Mary Ann kept the girl apart, within a magic circle of hardly contrived domesticity. So anxious was she to keep Lotta's actions modest that when she saw how she put her hands in the pockets of the little Irish suit as she sang, Mary Ann sewed them up—only to have the tiny actress, foiled in her sure business, run weeping from the stage, so that they had to be ripped open.

Almost every year Mrs. Crabtree took Lotta to San Francisco and tried to get her a toe hold on that crowded stage. Once they got as far as a billing in the famed American Theatre. Dr. Robinson, in the audience, hurried to the manager's room, and the next night his daughter Sue replaced the Crabtree child in the act. When another chance came, it was nothing but a walk-on; Lotta had only to come out on an empty stage and put a bottle on a table. But she performed this with an uproarious pantomime ending in a handspring into the wings, which stole the show. Nor would Lotta leave the challenge of San Francisco now. She was entering her teens; she clenched her two small fists in embattled anger, and began to batter her way through the obstacles put in her path by all the fellow professionals jealous each of his own slippery footing.

At first she could only get a chance as an attraction in

auction rooms, performing on a packing case or barrel head. She took day-by-day engagements, along the water front; she worked up to weekly contracts in saloons with dubious upstairs rooms, in third-rate theaters, then in second-rate, always with her mother hovering watchfully at hand. Only the miners in from the hills knew and cheered her vociferously. The crowds of the Embarcadero and the Barbary Coast were another, a duller and more vicious breed; her innocent mirth, her childlike sweetness were wasted on them. But San Francisco was not wasted upon Lotta. She missed nothing in the fermenting, violently contrasted, many-colored seaport. Its characters, its sights and sounds, were all to enrich her wondrous gift of mimicry, which in time enabled her to speak or sing, to strut or weep as any of a hundred souls in one tiny body.

When at last she made "the big time," she was still the hardest-working girl in California. Often she was billed in two theaters at once, and must dash from one to the other, changing costumes, parts, personalities, like the quicksilver that she was. Financial success, by the standards of a young variety entertainer, was already at hand, yet she and her mother, her young brothers, her father whenever he turned up, lived in cheap lodging houses, ate frugally, dressed severely. Off-stage the beautiful young girl's costume was always dark serge; she never owned a silk dress until she came of age. The spoiled and sharp-eyed cities of the East called her; she played Pittsburgh and Philadelphia, Boston and Chicago, and at last New York and even London. She took the shopworn plays of the times and broke them in her fingers like old boxes, to let loose a jeweled flood of extravagance, song, and laughter. She shattered every hoary rule of the stage—and why not, since she was queen of it? At the age of eighteen.

And still she was the clear-eyed little maid the miners had applauded. After the play was over, in her rooms she took a bowl of milk and crackers and went to bed. The news hawks quartered her every movement, for a love interest. She was briefly engaged to a young army officer, who died, and that was just all the reporters could scare up. In tribute to her art the Grand Duke Alexis presented her with a diamond necklace and bracelets. But what wealthy admirer did not shower her with jewels, which she never wore?

And then, at the age of forty-four, still the toast of the nineties, Lotta Crabtree left the stage forever. She still looked incredibly young, danced supple as a girl, sang with a fresh voice. But she had, practically without a rest, poured out her gifts in the theater for thirty years. More than any one performer, she had broken the old mold of English comedy and lifted the native American folk art of minstrelsy into a place of permanent honor on the stage. No one doubted that Lotta was financially free to retire, able to do what she pleased. And what she pleased was to live the family life she had never known in childhood. Her mother and father and her two brothers dwelt with her on a secluded New Jersey estate. There she delighted to raise race horses; she loved them, she said, "for their gameness. I love to see the beautiful things flashing by, mile after mile, and all without apparent effort."

So, to the public, the years of her youth had flashed. Her indomitable vitality lingered; she outlived all her family.

Retiring to her own hotel in Boston, she faced solitude, she who had known that headiest of unions—that being one with the audience, when the laughter and tears of the spectators become the real lines, fed to them over the footlights by their favorite, sometimes with no more than a gesture or look. This is the real drama, that ends only in that thrilling crisis, the wild release of applause, wave upon thundering wave, a storm before which the artist seems to bend helplessly, smiling almost as though to beg them stop.

They say that the aging and still lovely Lotta, there in the hotel where she lived by herself, used to put on at last the jewels she had never worn in youth, and so in tardy brilliance go down to dinner, alone and lonely. For she, the darling of the public, had never had the stellar role in woman's private life. For memories of men who had really loved her, she must turn back to the Forty-Niners. They were gone now, the men who were lusty when she was a child, the lovers of her enduring innocence, the luckless whose claims had never panned out, those others ready to chuck in their hand, give up, clear out, who had stayed on to see Lotta Crabtree dance and, sparked again to courage by that reviving joy, had struck it right at last and struck it rich. They were gone, for she was old now, but they were not forgotten. When in 1924 death lowered a slow curtain on her bright career, it was discovered that the Crabtree estate exceeded four million dollars—all of it left to the public, her public, that had so loved her. And something else was found, put away among her cherished possessions, dearest of them all—a box that when the lid was lifted proved full of golden nuggets.

Tracks West

How you and I, Mark, have drunk of the West together—
you driving the car as though it had stirrups and you could
set spurs to it! And all that wide waste of splendor under
a taut blue arch of sky was not empty for us, as many find
it, but brilliantly peopled. For you always knew where Red
Cloud had camped or Geronimo raided; you knew the sites
of those sudden bloody battles that befell when federal
troops riding out into the morning, guidons fluttering, met
the red men in ambush. In the grand panorama of the Civil
War, the military actions in our Southwest were minuscule,
but you knew them by heart, down to the last brave and
forgotten lieutenant. In that field you wrote the thesis for
your master's degree, beautifully pared of footnotes, smelling not of the lamp but of creosote bush and purple sage.

For, though you are so well trained as a historian, you
scorn the dryly academic, the approach through tortuous
interpretation by trend to this or that economic or so-
ciologic implication. Yours, as you cheerfully put it, is
"history for the hell of it." And here, as in all our long and

happy flights into the American West, I am with you. I'll
go a bit farther. I'll pick a piece of history that strikes my
fancy, and on that springboard take a leap into the possible.
There is truth, you'll agree, in a tale as well as in a record.

❦

W HEN I was a small boy, I thought there was no
other boy whose system so much required that he
ride on trains. Once I had put my lips to the
smoky intoxication of travel by rail, I was a slave to it for
life. I felt the craving in my bed at night, when I lay hearing
the long whistle of the B. and O.—going places. Early I
could recite the list of the converging railroads that head
into Chicago, and I could have told you where each one
led away. I would begin with the Père Marquette, which
took me to Grandfather's over in Michigan, and box the
compass right around, through the Grand Trunk, the Lake
Shore, the Big Four, the Nickelplate, the Monon, the Wa-
bash, the Rock Island, the Burlington, the Santa Fe, the
Great Western, the Union Pacific, the Milwaukee St. Paul,
and the Soo Line. Standing chest-deep in prairie dock and
mullein along the embankment, I would watch the lengthy
rumbling dragon of the freights roll past, blazoned with
these names and even stranger ones—the Boston and Maine,

the Central of Georgia, the Lackawanna, the Missouri
Pacific—till it wagged its caboose tail at me and vanished
into the sunset.

It wasn't just that I liked the lickety-split and the toot
and bustle of train travel. Even then I perceived that the
shining rails probe into the heart of our continent, and bring
forth its secrets. As I schemed and dreamed of trains taking
me to all of America, so they brought to me hints of the
part I longed for most, the greatest, the western part. Into
our station would come laboring a big black locomotive
hoary with the ice of a blizzard encountered far out on the
Nebraska prairies, so that I shivered with that distant cold.
Or, on blistering summer days, I heard the bellowing of
cattle penned in their cars, and I thought I could smell the
dust of the Texas Panhandle and see the cowboys riding by,
easy as kings in the saddle.

I haven't changed. The biggest day in every year is the
day when I wake up out on the sagebrush plains, in a west-
bound train, and begin to watch for the Rockies to show
their white-feathered war bonnets over the rim of the world.
In the observation car, I take the end chair, and sit spell-
bound, watching the endlessly converging and dwindling
rails. That is our past which we are forever leaving. And, as
I longed once for all wide America, so I yearn backward
now to the boundless, unwritten, unconquered America
that the searching rails found out.

I met the other day an old woman who had been present
at the driving of the Golden Spike—a little girl then in a
wide felt hat, trying to peep between the grownups; she,
and most people, think that the great moment in the rail-

road story is that conclusive one. But in our beginnings lies
all our future greatness at its purest. I choose, in railroad
history, the year 1852, when the government authorized,
under the direction of the Honorable the Secretary of War,
Mr. Jefferson Davis, six surveys "to ascertain," in the words
of the Thirty-third Congress, "the most practicable and
economical route for a railroad from the Mississippi River
to the Pacific Ocean." Obedient, six expeditions started
forth, from the Canadian border to the Mexican, hunting
a way, through passes, over canyons, across deserts, among
Apaches, Blackfeet, Piutes, Shoshones, for a young nation
to build a one-track line (that's all we could see then, all
we could afford) to link our old shores with our new, our
West with East.

Where they went we have double-tracked now. The Great
Northern, the Northern Pacific, the Union Pacific, the
Santa Fe, the Southern Pacific—they were all there because
of a few bands of men, soldiers, surveyors, engineers, map-
makers. Among these useful members went a sprinkling of
scientists, odd birds boldly flying ahead of the culture they
represented—geologists to help the engineers and look for
signs of mineral wealth, naturalists to collect the animals,
living or fossil, botanists to hunt for timber for the ties that
would be laid, and to pick up by the way all the fresh and
pungent things here growing which had never been noted
before.

Now what these expeditions did and saw is all recorded in
a dozen volumes, bound in quarto as "the Pacific Railway
Reports." They are a collector's item with lovers of West-
erniana; you pick them up, an odd volume at a time, in

dusty bookshops. They are dry, as the desert itself, unless
you search between the lines for springs of once living adventure.

A writer knows, by a quickening tug like that in water-
witching, when he has found in the bare facts an imaginable
truth. The following facts come out of one of those crumbling quarto volumes with the quaint steel engravings in it.
But the original colors are faded, and I have had to restore
them. For this there is no need of apology, since the most
stirring thing about our favorite national legend, the saga
of the Far West, is that it is all true. And men of the professions are apt to follow in one another's traces, and ways of
thought, so that I am sure of the nature of my captain, of
my doctor, and as for the young scientist, he is surprisingly
like myself. For he was a botanist too, trained too at Harvard, but under the great Asa Gray (whose foremost student
was my first professor). His name was Caleb Winthrop,
and we will strike his trail at the hundredth meridian, the
end of the thirty-ninth *jornada* out of Fort Smith, Arkansas.
A *jornada*, as Caleb had learned in Professor Longfellow's
Spanish class at Harvard College, means "the task for the
day," the stint.

But now the sonorous tones of the poet-professor, the
Georgian serenity of Massachusetts Hall, were half a continent, another life away from this mournful ocean of sagebrush and grass. And out here, in the buffeting of the wind,
under the September sun of the Llano Estacado, a *jornada*
meant, in the language of Vincente, the Mexican-Indian
interpreter, a day's journey on a trail never trodden before
unless by buffalo or Indians. It meant all you could accom-

plish from sun to sun, all you could stand of the dust raised
by the mounts of the troop of Dragoons, of three officers,
three railway engineers, the topographer, the Army surgeon,
and by the mules which dragged the reeling *carretelas.* All
you could endure of buffalo flies and saddle sores, of the
everlasting boasting drawl of Texans, of the gray judging
eyes of Captain Stephen Demerrit.

In each twilight, as they lifted off the saddles, Vincente
would say in his singsong Mexican Spanish (quite unlike
Professor Longfellow's), "Each *jornada* is but a day, *señor.*
Yesterday has gone by, and you cannot live tomorrow till
it comes. Today you have done what you could do; what
you could not, was not God's will."

That thirty-ninth day began, I find on reference to the
meteorological notes, with a change in the weather. Autumn
had come in a night, though there were here no New England maples to proclaim it. The shimmering heat waves that
had kept the horizons queasy were suddenly gone, and in
the sharpened air the far-off mesas strode a league and a
league nearer, to stand clear as steps cut out of stone, one
lifting beyond another, the flat tops tawny with bunch grass,
the faces fallen in talus, like the ruins of some shattered
temple. All the survey noted the sense of rising; the ground
under their saddles, under the horse hoofs, was feeling the
long rollers, the dead swell of some far-off storm, the earth-
storm of the approaching Rockies. Air, suddenly, was a song
in the lungs, was a falconer's fist that tossed a quartering
hawk aloft, aslant, was a whistling sword that slew all the
hosts of grass, then let them live again. Streams that had
wandered, thin and dirty, pitched forward now with a living

clatter. Their fringe of cottonwoods whispered panic, told scare stories of Indians, who might not now be far.

And that day closed as all before had closed, with the Captain taking a meridianal observation on the stars. All day the Captain bore himself like the West Pointer he was, rode like a centaur, led his men with a wordless awareness of each of them; wherever he was, he seemed, in effect, to be at the head of the column, yet if he rode there, his will was felt behind the last mule-skinner, driving the column home like a wedge into wilderness. When at dusk camp was made, in some cottonwood grove, under some crumbling river bluff, or in sheer sagebrush emptiness, he unpacked his astronomical instruments and became what he most deeply was—a mariner in space, captain of more than a little band of dusty men, rather of our great ship of state now headed toward open and unknown wastes which he must chart, and so bear all a pilot's lonely burden.

Now to the men he appeared a martinet, for if his site for triangulation was troubled by a gleam of campfires, then they must be extinguished and removed three hundred feet, lest the brief earthly sparks of snapping sage wood, or the smoky orange of buffalo chips, should rival the chill pure light falling from Vega. And first a deep circular trench had to be dug around this sacred triangulation point, leaving the instruments on an isolated column of earth, so that the stamping of the mounts, and even the steps of the men, should not cause some distant world to tremble in the transit. Once he had stepped over the trench, Captain Demerrit was not to be spoken to. He wished to hear no voice but that of his recorder. "Two minutes," floated the

chanting bass warningly through the darkness, and with a
sensitive hand the Captain adjusted the azimuth micrometer
screw. "One minute . . . thirty seconds . . . fifteen seconds,"
then the ringing cry of *"Time!"* In that instant Captain
Demerrit bisected Polaris with the middle wire of his transit,
and forced the universe to tell him where he was. Which
was this evening, as I have said, precisely on the hundredth
meridian, west longitude. West, the Captain meant, of
Greenwich, England. But west an infinity from Harvard
College, and from the Second Unitarian Church in Boston
where Caleb Winthrop had early learned a gentle morality
from the Reverend Ralph Waldo Emerson.

> "Hast thou named all the birds without a gun?
> Loved the wood rose, and left it on its stalk?"

Caleb had been taught to recite that soon after he learned
the Lord's Prayer, and in it lay all this youthful scientist's
innocent credo. I have said that, oddly enough, he greatly
resembles myself when young. So that I know what he felt
about that vast virgin territory, and how, riding out ahead
to collect new plants, he would look back, aghast to see how
fast the troopers' mounts, the *carretela* wheels, the hoofs of
the cattle train were coming on, to crush, relentless and
unknowing, what he did not swiftly save. And I know the
elixir in his veins when he stopped to lift out of the untram-
pled earth the wild gilia. (For one "wood rose"—and a few
duplicates for the Smithsonian, the British Museum, the
Jardin des Plantes—were permitted to him to pluck.)

I came on that very specimen gathered on this day of their
thirty-ninth *jornada,* in the Gray Herbarium at Harvard,

when I was a student there, at Caleb's age. I remember the date, the fifteenth of September, on the collector's label, because it was the very day, the first of the new fall term, when I stood gazing at this dried and faded scrap of our primeval western flora. In this boundless cemetery of pressed plants, each bearing on its little white tombstone of a label the date and place of its collection, I was wandering headily, far beyond the boundaries of my student's assignment, into provinces and eras past when all my world was young. The man who collected this, I saw, was one I had been taught to revere, by my professors of botany, as a titan whose elder spirit still walked these corridors, wafting through them the romance of our Homeric age of scientific exploration. So to my eyes the sere and two-dimensional flower glued to the sheet regained its faded tints, the delicate tension of freshness in its petals, the perfume which scented a wind long blown by.

And to my sympathetic mind comes clearly now the mood of Caleb, on the wind-blown Llano. I understand how an ideal of nature—existing, for him, principally to be studied by the comprehending and reverent—gleamed like a guiding star in his lens—because so it has shone in mine. By it he could always orient himself tranquilly, for until now, until the bright morning of the fortieth day out from Fort Smith, never had the solid ground beneath his feet been made to shudder by the approach of violence.

Vincente was the first to pick up Indian sign. It was a big party, he said, plenty horses, and women's moccasin prints pressed deep with the weight of the burden baskets. Then the Dragoons' horses caught the smell of the Indian mounts, and began to whinny and fret. The Texans sat even straighter in their saddles, drawing a shorter rein. Captain Demerrit leaned forward in the saddle, touched his mare to a trot, and gained the head of the column in silence. Young Mr. Winthrop, student of the author of *Hiawatha*, nourished on the *Last of the Mohicans*, said to old Dr. Marceau, who rode at his side, "Comanches, do you think they'll be? I hope the soldiers won't want to get rough with them."

"No fear," said the surgeon dryly. "Our orders are to enlist the co-operation of all the tribes. You forget, in your posy-picking, we're surveying for a railroad. Trouble is just what we don't want."

Then ahead, on a rise, they saw the wigwam village, the lodgepoles forking from the apex of the walls of painted buffalo hide in savage alphabet against the bald blue sky. They smelled the bitter reek of fires that have cooked meat and still are smoldering with the drippings. Abruptly a dry arroyo brought them all to a halt, and down the opposite slope came riding a band of Kiowas, their lance points all akimbo, bristling and glistening in the sun, their feather bonnets tossing restless as thunderbirds, their mounts, checked by a hard bridle at the draw's edge, nickering and striking at the air with their forelegs. The voices of the women running among the wigwams came like the crying of a wild gaggle of fowl, above the hoarse raven voices of the braves.

"Mr. Winthrop," floated back the Captain's cool tone, "will you have the goodness to order our interpreter forward with a flag of truce?"

Caleb, his heart thumping, put this into Spanish; Dr. Marceau leaned from his saddle with a clean handkerchief; Vincente fixed it to a proffered ramrod and rode forward, the sign of amity fluttering dove-white in the Llano wind.

All the Kiowas seemed to comprehend the international symbol at once. The braves, the women, even the raving curs, fell as suddenly silent as frogs when a stone is flung in their swamp. The survey party watched tensely, as the half-breed faced the full bloods and began to pound out and point and flicker the sign language of the plains tribes. Riding back at the quick trot of success, he spoke to Winthrop in his Mexican Spanish, and the young scientist, in the accents of Boston, reported to the Captain that the Indians did not wish to fight; that they hoped the soldiers would not use their guns, and that the whites might show their friendliness by camping in the village. All this Demerrit accepted in a nod; he gave the command of "Forward!" and the little troop, followed by the lowing Arkansas cattle, dustily crossed this western Rubicon.

"Indians are terrible enemies," Dr. Marceau observed to Caleb, while the Kiowas dashed laughing and whooping among the jostled survey party, "but so are they terrible friends."

Caleb hardly heard him. Nothing in Cooper's romances had readied him for the splendor of these fierce children of the desert. There was little red to be seen about them, save a gleam of naked thighs above the leather leggings bound with silver buckles, and the streak of vermilion grease down the parting of the hair. Their faces were painted yellow, their fine blue blankets fluttered from their shoulders; the

red, white, and blue feathers of their bonnets, trailed in
queues to the horses' flanks. Flat bands of Mexican silver
bound their bare arms, and great hoops of brass swung from
their ears. Their bows were studded with nails of brass and
silver, and the arrows lisped and rattled in the quivers of
white wolfskin. This, this, exulted Caleb, was the ultimate
in primitive glory, the culminating species in the fauna of
aboriginal America!

As the party entered the village, he saw for the first
time in his life women bare above the girdle, and scientifi-
cally noted that no sensual admiration crossed his mind,
only a pride in their proud bronze freedom. He bravely
disregarded the sunny stench of the greased bodies; the
kicks, at which the milling curs bared needle fangs; the aspen
pole, guarded by a screeching hag, from which three scalps
mingled their black hairs helplessly in the wind. A surge of
respect, almost of awe, uplifted him as he glimpsed beyond
Captain Demerrit the advancing figure of the chief—a man
so splendid in his own bodily right that he seemed to disdain
the trappings of his warriors. Blue-beaded moccasins and a
white twist of cloth about the thighs were all his clothing;
in his hand he held a pipe of red steatite with carved and
feathered stem, and on a silver chain a great cross of silver
glittered with his breathing against his naked chest. Facing
him, the Captain looked slight, thought Caleb. What were
they all doing here, anyway, he demanded of himself in
sudden anger—invading with the hideous threat of "progress" this self-sufficient kingdom of the free?

As the chief began to speak, in slow, deep Kiowa, all that
Caleb had ever read in Schoolcraft's *Indian Tribes* told him

what must be meant by this native oratory—the moving grandeur, the stately welcome, of what Caleb had been taught to call "the vanishing red man." He was like the orb —it came emotionally to Caleb—of some full-bodied sun going down in cloudless splendor, touching and illuminating the horizon. And then behind the shoulder of the chief, Caleb, unbelieving, saw emerge the slim crescent of a white woman, with tragic blue eyes and a torrent of auburn hair. With one hand she held the hand of a three-year-old boy, with the other she covered her breast.

The woman, the chief, the Captain, Vincente talking to the big Kiowa with his hands, the handsome child—they are all there, in Executive Document Number 91, printed by order of the House of Representatives. The item is set down with the tight-lipped, dry-eyed compassion of Captain Demerrit. For men of action do not record their emotions for print; they put down only data, dry as that pressed specimen of gilia. But is there one of us not wistful, when we dwell upon such traces of the past, for the living light, the singing blood, the heat of that long-gone day? History, really, is what you choose to make of the facts, and I am choosing, by your leave, to read between, as well as straight along, the lines of this Pacific Railway Report.

There I perceive how little Caleb Winthrop—the future Dr. Winthrop, Linnaean Professor of Botany at Harvard College—knew, at twenty-one, about women. He had a mother whom he took so for granted he never saw her as anything else. He had a girl, like any Harvard student, to meet in the dusk under Brattle Street lilacs. He was wholly unprepared for the woman who stepped that night out of the shadow of the cottonwoods, as he walked by them toward the tent he shared with the doctor. It was in rapid Spanish that she talked to him there in the dark, and all the time he listened, horror growing, he was remembering her captive beauty in sunlight, that he had watched all during the powwow. So shaken had he been by the sight that he feared it might have been through lapses of his, as translator between Vincente and the Captain, that the negotiations with the Kiowa chief had gone so badly, had ended on a note of hostility. For he had been half lost in the woman's pleading gaze, so that suddenly the chief noticed this, and ordered her away. In that command, he had abruptly shown that he was her master. To the young New Englander who never before had seen a woman obey a man with a look of fear, black depths opened, and when he looked up again at the brilliant circle of Kiowas they were altered, their animal grace became brute strength, their eyes now cruel and cunning, and on the chief's breast the great silver cross, he saw, must be the loot of some nobly founded mission, as the woman was of some butchered household.

And this she now told him. As my Pacific Report tells me, on page 31: "She said that her name was José Maria; that she was from Rio de Naces; had been captured by the Kiowas when she was twenty and had lived with them seven years. Her beautiful boy is the son of the chief, but she wishes to leave her hard masters and accompany us, in the hope of again reaching her home." That could only be managed, she passionately urged upon Caleb, by her purchase from the chief, and she admitted, since he already was suspicious and angered with the whites, that the price would be great.

When Caleb, in his shy young way, was kind, she flung herself upon him, sobbing.

Now were the far cool planetary principles of Caleb's life sent reeling down his darkened heavens. With hot blood, with borrowed shames and angers burning in him, he sought out Captain Demerrit. The Captain, said a sentry, abruptly barring his way, was not to be disturbed. This was the hour at which he took his nightly observations on the stars.

On the gravestone of General Stephen Demerrit, in the Soldier's National Cemetery at Gettysburg, are carved the lines he loved best in life: *The starry heavens above me, the sense of duty within me.* So you may guess what he said to young Caleb Winthrop, when at last he stepped back from his preoccupation with Ursa Minor and listened to the young man's furious story.

"All very well, Mr. Winthrop, and all very sorry. But my duty is quite clear. If she were an American citizen, there might be some question; she is a Mexican national. As to purchasing her freedom, the Secretary of War, I may inform you, has allotted to this survey the sum of forty thousand dollars. That must cover every expenditure, and only a fraction can go to trading goods. You saw for yourself that our presents were not enough to please the chief; we have still fifteen hundred miles to go, through one insatiable tribe after another."

How many human feelings have beaten, bruised, against the bars of military necessity! Caleb, with all the moral strength he had ever learned, tried again, but Captain Demerrit was short and final.

"Impossible. I have no authorization to purchase Indians' captives. This is the chief's woman, Mr. Winthrop, and to attempt to buy her would rouse him to dangerous hostility."

Night covers many things; the stars are very far and faint, and sometimes they are clouded. On the Llano, as under the elms, it may hide the sweetest things and the bitterest. It brings us all its nightmares and its inviting visions. If all is well, it brings us sleep, but to the tortured it can bring a kind of madness. Nor is there any torture like that of untried youth when he has lost his way by his stars, when all that seemed fairest is suddenly revealed at its most hideous, when the strange woman troubles the blood, and honor demands the impossible.

So, before the light, the sleepless Caleb like a sleepwalker threw back his blankets and stood up. Across the tent he saw that Dr. Marceau lay still. Out on the Llano a burrowing owl gave his high mellow quaver, and through the open tent flap a pale sunrise filled the east. It showed Caleb the dark familiar silhouette of Marceau's Army pistol in its holster hanging from the tent pole. The boy had never before picked up a weapon with intent to use it if he must, but the deathy touch of the cold metal went through his hot veins, steeling him in his purpose. He had no plan to kill, only to bargain at gun's point; a thunder like escaping hoofbeats pounded in his temples as though the woman were already mounted behind him.

"Boy," came the quiet voice of the surgeon out of the gloom, "that weapon isn't loaded. And anyway, the hand of a man who hasn't slept all night isn't steady enough to shoot."

Old Dr. Winthrop, they say, when he entertained his classes with tales of western exploration used to tell that story on himself with a chuckle. It isn't the ivy at my alma mater that keeps the walls so green; it is the well-rooted, the youthfully fresh wisdom that clings to them still, left by the teachers who have passed through them. Some of that, no doubt, was gained on the Llano, that dawn which opened the forty-first *jornada,* when the seasoned Army surgeon talked sense to the shaken young man. Thus, as we learn from our teachers, so they have learned from theirs, and what we come to know, about the stars and the plants and the mysterious ways of man is laid down, piece after piece, across the wastes of our ignorance, as the shining rails came to pierce the desert.

Those rails, I think, as I watch them dwindling behind us, have brought much more than they took away. They took away the stretches of blue gilia, and brought us wheat, which is also a flower, and gives us this day our daily bread. They took the Kiowas in all their painted splendor, and ended too their raids, and the slavery and shame that woman knew. If she was left helpless behind, as the railroad survey went driving through, that is because civilization—a slow and halting progress, really—leaves many victims by the wayside, bits of the day's task that could not be accomplished because it was not God's will. For each of us, the doctor, the engineer, the scientist, can accomplish daily but one *jornada.* Yet where that survey party crawled, our great trains fly now, crying their long clarion greeting to the future, and when across the land you hear it, that's America on its way.

The Ballad of
Cynthia Ann

I offer you now, Mark, a story that you and I have often discussed, fascinated. The Texans, to whom it belongs, are delighted with it too. It speaks for itself, I think, and yet I can't help saying a word or two under my breath here, because I don't think the good people who have inherited it quite perceive its full meaning. That would shock them, if they did.

For a great many Americans are not yet ready to believe that the worth of a man cannot be told by the color of his skin. And this results in rash and sometimes cruel acts which are grave impediments to the work you and your fellows are doing out there in Asia. The white men in the story that follows were sure they were right and generally kind, at great pains to themselves. But my heroine, in her wonderful savage way, rose above even their earnest goodness.

Not until all of us rise above the walls of race—built by our own stubbornness—will we all be free. And freedom—dangerous though it is because it gives our fate into our hands—for all men is surely a first essential for total peace.

THIS is an old tale, and not a pretty one; it is a true tale, a real "Western," although it wouldn't go on TV. It sounds to me like a ballad sung to a banjo— the ballad of Cynthia Ann.

But Cynthia Ann, fleeing us all on the thunder of Comanche hoofs, is no part of a sentimental ditty. By all accounts, she was a very pretty little girl. One of about eighteen children at Parker's Fort on the Navasota River, she was the kind men pick out for a tweak of the curls or a joking word—even those grim pioneers whose eyes saw less of the beauty around them than visions of the day when the Lord would drive their enemies out of the land. The women, trying to describe her afterwards, said she had blue eyes and light hair—flax-flower eyes, I fancy, wheat-straw hair that curled, as a child's will in hot weather, softly at the temples where the veins show blue in the porcelain flesh. The women would remember that flesh with burning pity. Cynthia Ann was in her ninth year on the last day of Fort Parker, which was May 19, 1836.

That day dawned warm, then turned to a regular east-Texas hot spring morning. For a while the women in Parker's Fort could hear their men's voices out in the fields in the shimmering heat waves. Then the voices drifted away down the long furrows. The women sought cool footing

(shoes were for Sunday) as they went about their tasks.
Rachel Plummer moved languidly, eight months gone with
child. Old Granny Parker (eighty-odd) drove the flies from
the parchment of her face.

The people in Parker's Fort numbered only thirty-five
souls. Patriarch of them all was Elder John Parker, who had
led his people—the Parkers, the Plummers, the Nixons and
other neighbors from back East—across the Red River into
the Canaan of Texas soil. And he was a God-fearing, "Two-
seed" Baptist, and his son the Reverend James Parker
walked in the ways of the Lord also, and so did his brothers
Isaac and Silas and Benjamin. And they took unto themselves wives, all except young Benjamin, and begat children.
And the names of their children were Rachel and Sara and
James and John and the like—all Bible names. All except
Cynthia Ann, daughter of Silas, the son of Elder John. Her
name, whether her mother knew it or not, was Greek. For
"Cynthia" is one of the titles of Artemis, goddess of the
moon and protectress of maidens.

But to protect her now there wasn't a soldier left in the
fort. The Republic of Texas had pulled them all out some
weeks ago, now that the Indian frontier had retreated a
hundred miles to the west. Nobody that morning was thinking of Indians; why should they?

Then, suddenly, out of the prairie heat waves—they were
there: Comanches and Kiowas, some afoot, some sitting
ponies. The braves weren't yelling or brandishing their
shields of buffalo hide. They were just staring in silence—
a long, deadly stillness. Even the buffalo horns and the eagle
plumes of their headdresses hardly stirred. Their fourteen-

foot lances were motionless as a grove of dead saplings, only the feathers near the tips trembling a little in the south wind.

Benjamin Parker, Cynthia Ann's youngest uncle, went out to meet them and play for time—enough for Mrs. Sarah Nixon, Cynthia's cousin, to run for the fields with the alarm. Ben talked as long as he could, then came into the fórt to say the Indians showed by sign they wanted beef. There was none, so he went back to temporize. He was the first to die. They clubbed, speared, and scalped him under the aghast eyes at the portholes in the log stockade.

Now the yells broke. The mounted Indians dashed their ponies in a noose around the fort. They swept up young Mrs. Elizabeth Kellogg; Rachel Plummer, a child in her arms and another inside her, was dragged away by her hair along the ground. The folding gate of wooden slabs yielded to the blows of the hostiles. As it burst in, one scream tore the throats of the ten women, the fifteen children. With them were only four men—old Elder John, and Silas (Cynthia's father), and Robert Frost and his son Samuel. They had time for a single burst of firing, a single yell of triumph from Silas as a few Indians fell. Then all the men were overpowered, killed, stripped, and scalped.

Cynthia Ann heard her mother's voice urging her on, but she couldn't outrun those long coppery legs. A copper hand was in her hair; a hard arm scooped her up by her waist. Her own mother was forced to set her on a pony's back behind a mounted brave, and stand staring after her as she was borne away.

For now from the fields came the rest of the men, crouching as they ran. They were armed, though short of bullets and powder, which were mostly in the fort. Their line of fire was a ragged popping; these were farmers who never before had shot anything more dangerous than a snake or hawk. But they turned back the Comanche charge, and then another, and gained time for the children and women to scatter like quail in the brush down by the Navasota's banks.

The Indians didn't charge again. They were dealing with the milch cows now, filling them full of arrows as so many pincushions. The farmers could hear the beasts bellowing. Soon they saw the red and yellow flames war-dancing in the standing crops.

Deep in the woods the men began hunting for their families, children for their parents. These refugees were many starving days from safety. The shoeless had to walk all the way on bleeding feet. Yet they all made it back to the eastern settlements. The wounded made it, a woman with child made it. Old Granny Parker, speared and left for dead, played possum till darkness—she made it too. Three nursing mothers somehow brought their babes through the flight; Nature wrung the milk out of their gaunt flesh to nourish the frail hopes they carried.

Wouldn't you think they'd had enough of Fort Parker? Then you don't know your own American ancestors. For practically all of these people returned to the fort in a short time. They buried the bones, picked clean by wolves and vultures, of their dead. They planted another crop that year. They begot and bore and raised more children. They brought more Bibles with them, and read aloud together the covenant of Jehovah with those who keep His commandments.

And now the heathen wilderness began to give up some of those ravished away. Elizabeth Kellogg was the first to return. Unbroken in spirit, she had given such a thrashing to a squaw who was beating her that the Ketchaw Indians admiringly named her "Brave Woman." They sold her for $150 in trading goods to some Delawares (always allies of the whites) who brought her home. Rachel Plummer, that same autumn, was purchased by Santa Fe traders and brought back to her husband. Of her son Pratt, taken from her early in captivity, she never lived to hear news. Yet seven years later he was turned over by friendly Indians to the soldiers at Fort Gibson.

But the Indians had taken Cynthia Ann to a place that no honest white man ever saw—and lived. It is the center of the whirlwind, the ancient and most secret hide-out of the Comanches. It is the lost and inaccessible valley where a stream comes down, between war-paint canyon walls, from the high Llano Estacado through the break of the cap rock. That stream was called the Rio de las Lenguas—"the river of tongues"—for the many tongues that were spoken here: Kiowa, Comanche, Wichita, Jicarilla, Mescalero, a cawing Babel like ravens and geese and whooping cranes all calling together. The Comancheros, white renegades who rode out from New Mexico to trade here for stolen cattle and horses, with a cruel poetry named this spot—where women were sold among the tribes, where children were reft from

the clutch of their mothers, and girls knew brutal hands—
the Valle de las Lágrimas.

Into that blackness vanished Cynthia Ann.

Years had passed, and Colonel Len Williams, with his
fellow trader, Stoat, and the Delaware guide, Jack Harry,
were parleying with Pahuaka's band of Comanches down
by the bank of the Canadian River. Heat and excitement
fevered the Colonel's impatience. Best let the more stoic
Stoat negotiate. For the Colonel himself hadn't a doubt
of the identity of that blond girl of thirteen among the
Comanches. Promptly he had offered to buy her freedom;
proudly Pahuaka replied that members of his tribe were
not for sale. The Colonel then asked to speak with the
girl, and received the startling answer that the chief would
have to get the permission of her mother and father.

Now the girl, in Indian dress, walked slowly out of the
group and toward him, her eyes on the ground. At the
Colonel's feet she sat down, as a modest Comanche girl
does before a man, tucked her legs under her skirt, and
folded her hands in her lap—the incarnation of obedient
attention.

The Colonel spoke, coolly, kindly. Her family had been
hunting her for years. Her playmates remembered her. Her
place waited for her, and a warm welcome. And he promised
to raise any sum for her ransom that the Indians might ask.

She raised her eyes. And what he saw was nothing he had
ever seen before in the gaze of any woman, least of all in
the look of a young white girl. In that long glance he saw
the Llano—the endless level of the high-lifted short-grass
plain, where there is nothing from dawn to sunset to give

back an echo. Even the blue of those eyes was like the Llano sky, that arches over the buffalo grass and the curlew lakes, and is unchanging, beyond recollection or fear of pity.

He dropped his own startled gaze. It's no use, he knew. There's nothing we can do with this. Let us go.

Yes, they went, and they let her go back—back to the blanket. For there is no fugitive so difficult to pursue as the freed will of a woman—unless it is a Comanche.

The tribe was, in those days, the whirlwind itself, possessed of the greatest horsemen in history. Greater, said old cavalry officers, than Arabs or Bedouins or Cossacks. It was they, perhaps, who were first of the red men to master horses —beasts descended from strayed or stolen mounts of the Spaniards. From the moment that the Comanche leaped to the back of that mustang, he changed from the clumsiest Indian afoot into the "red knight of the plains."

With horses, the Comanches' striking power was fluid as the Llano wind. The West Point style of cavalry charge was useless against a foe who could hang by his heels while galloping, and shoot arrows under the horse's neck so fast that he could keep eight of them in the air all the time. The Texas Ranger could get in at most three shots—one from a rifle and one each from a brace of pistols—before he had to reload. In the sixty seconds needed for that, a Comanche horseman could close in for the kill.

It was in horses that a Comanche counted his wealth; racing he thought the one sport worthy of a man. Squaws, too, rode like wild spirits of the air; they too could hang by their heels, vault up again to the saddle, or spring from one galloping steed to another. The horse lifted the Comanche woman from a beast of burden to a mate, mounted and proud and free, whose bride-price had been paid by her suitor in those very animals that made of him a red halfgod, a centaur out of myth. . . . That was how Peta Nakona, young chief of the Kwahadi band of Comanches, obtained Cynthia Ann from her red foster parents when she would have been about fifteen years old.

In 1851, some Texas travelers fell in with the Kwahadi band along the upper Canadian River. They stared long at the hair of the young chief's wife; it was straight as an Indian's, smelling of the lodge fires, but yellow, yellow. Her skin was tanned to leathery brown; in her eyes, when they questioned her, there was no gleam of recognition. Not even at the name of Cynthia Ann Parker. She was Preloch now (say the *ch* hard, as in the Scottish loch). No, she answered in Comanche, she had no desire to return to her white relatives, to leave her two swarthy little sons, and her good husband.

I know, I know. It doesn't fit at all with the ten-gallon legend. It's right in the script that any white woman would spurn the embrace of a no-account, red-handed, scalp-lifting Indian varmint. And the fair-haired girl is always rescued by the Lone Ranger.

All right. I'll play you the banjo tune for a minute—and I'll be telling the truth. That's just what happened.

The Kwahadi band—so went the Texan tune—had to be punished. They'd been raiding; the frontier was aflame. So, in December of 1860, forty-seven Rangers, under the command of Captain Sul Ross, took the field in vengeance. Joining them was a handful of settlers and cowboys, and twenty-three dragoons, fight-loving Irishmen. In all, they made a motley force of some eighty, in every kind of uniform or duds, on every sort of mount.

United in their enmity, these outfits had their own ways of fighting; when it came to scalp-lifting, you couldn't always tell a Texas settler from a Comanche; the dragoons shot squaws as soon as bucks. (Harsh truth drowns out the banjo.) And the Rangers had at last got Colt six-shooters. They were the first to use the Colt on the Comanches, and with it they turned the whole tide of Indian warfare. Now it was they, not the red centaurs, who charged, and their in-fighting was so close they powder-burned the coppery skins.

Thus, on the morning of December 19, the end was clear in the beginning, when the whites surprised the Kwahadi camp on the desolate banks of the Pease. It was the same end, of course, as that which had come to Fort Parker. The Comanches fled, as the Baptists had fled, larruping their wild-eyed ponies, toppling, under the leaden hail, sideways or backwards with a last crazy salute of upflung hands. Only one figure, crouched low on an iron-gray mount, was pacing the wind. She outraced the Rangers, all but outran the bullets, until at their whine around her ears she reined, plunging, and lifted high above her head a swaddled babe, hostage to surrender, pledge of her womanhood.

So they took her. Took her first to Camp Cooper, where the officers' wives were kindly pitying, and cooed over Tautaijah, the tiny red baby. They improved the Indian syllables into Topsannah, and declared it meant "Prairie Flower." (You know how we make up the Indian's poetry

for him, to fit our Longfellow notions.) To poor Cynthia
Ann Parker they showed every Christian charity—and met
the glare of Preloch, a caged female whose mate and cubs
were still out in the wild. Twice she stole a horse and with
her babe in her arms streaked as only a Comanche could
for the open. But the cavalry did its job; she was always
brought back. Everybody concerned was glad when Senator
(and Colonel) Isaac Parker came and took his niece and
her child away.

He brought her home, to the piny eastern part of Texas,
to her younger brother Dan Parker's house in Athens.

The state legislature was so good as to vote a pension to
Cynthia Ann. But it bought nothing that Preloch wanted
in this world. Nor could money save Topsannah when she
sickened. For as soon as she was weaned and began taking
white man's food, she wasted, and presently was laid beneath a stone.

Her mother did not long survive her. Some say she died
of sorrow, some that she starved herself to death. By 1864
she was buried in the old Fosterville cemetery. No doubt
they put a cedar by her head, to point the way to heaven.
No doubt they planted periwinkle; they usually do, on a
woman's grave, down South. Its kitten-eyed blue flowers
bring to mind the little girl who vanished a quarter-century
before, by the salt river of tongues, in the war-paint valley
of tears.

So ends the ballad, my ballad of Cynthia Ann. So, you
might think, ends the story. I point no moral to it; I lift
no finger to show any one way to salvation. Indeed, if you
look well at our history—look between the eyes at our con-

quest of the land, once all the red man's, you find yourself, like me, falling silent. All we can say is that out of that murder and rapine, out of that courage and struggle, came this, our nation. And in its history there's one more paragraph I must relate, which adds an envoy to my ballad.

You remember the two little sons she had, out in the whirlwind wilderness? The eldest, Quanah, was in battle where she was captured, and he escaped with the remnant of his people. At twenty-two he became the chief of the Kwahadi band, still the most bitter and intractable of all Comanches. Most of them agreed, by the Medicine Lodge Treaty of 1867, to come into the reservation. Not Quanah; he kept out on the Llano, leading the United States Army in circles after him. He is described as the most ferocious Indian ever encountered, by an officer who saw him lead a charge—a smoking six-shooter in his hand, bear-claw necklace at his throat, war bonnet streaming behind him, his face satanic with daubs of red and ocher.

And then—what gentling, south-wind spirit reached to him? What strangely prompted him, in 1875, suddenly to surrender? He brought his people down out of the plains, turned over all his arms, and settled with his band at the foot of the Wichita Mountains, in Indian Territory. He saw to it that every little Comanche went to school, to learn the white man's language and study in his books. Jovial, hospitable in the big house he built for his three wives and fifteen children, Quanah was fond of a good cigar and relished a fund of racy stories.

It's the last of the story, it's the end of the song—all the plaintive sorrow drowned in the sound of a big brass band.

It's 1905, on Pennsylvania Avenue in Washington, and that's Teddy Roosevelt's inaugural parade swinging down through the cheering throng, the flags, the gaudy music of "The Stars and Stripes Forever" and "Hail to the Chief," the white man's chief, the Rough Rider President. And in the parade are great chiefs of his red brothers, Chief Joseph of the Nez Perces and Quanah of the Comanches—Quanah, son of Cynthia Ann, her victory out of defeat.

Postscript

THUS, on a note of brassy harmony and common triumph, my parade swings out of sight. I have been happy, Mark, in putting together these pages as an answer to you, with the sense that I was marching at your side. It isn't so, of course; that is not the tramp of doubled footsteps that I hear, but the beat of my heart going out to you. For you, and all the other color-bearers of your generation, are stepping out into the future, where I may not long follow you. But above the multitudinous turmoil of the times, I see the flag borne on, lifted by the wind of our freedom, carried forward by those young, strong hands, beautiful in its bright pattern of truth and generosity, starred brilliantly with hope.

About the Author

In *Parade with Banners* Donald Culross Peattie writes of his country both as a naturalist and as a historian. Born on Midsummer Day in 1898, into a home where books and laughter, ideals and affection nourished a strong faith in the American spirit, he was later trained for a career in the natural sciences at Harvard (which has awarded him two degrees with honors).

While working as a botanist in the Department of Agriculture in Washington, he married Louise Redfield, the novelist. Soon his love of nature found expression in books which brought him fame—*An Almanac for Moderns, Singing in the Wilderness,* and others.

Motoring about his native land to discover its beauties, with his wife and sometimes his three sons, he came to look ever deeper into its history. Out of these researches came such books as *Forward the Nation, Journey into America,* and *American Heartwood.* Invited by *The Reader's Digest* in 1943 to become a "roving editor," he found his audience increased by millions, and his travels taking him to many lands.

At home in his study in Santa Barbara, California, he finds that such far journeys serve to sharpen his focus as a writer about his own country. And when his second son, serving as an officer of USIA in a remote corner of the Far East, called on his father for a book to stir our spirits to meet the challenge of these times, Mr. Peattie answered with this volume in which, as he puts it, he lifts "a few of our American banners."

This book was set in

Electra and Caslon types by

The Haddon Craftsmen.

The paper is Perkins and Squier Company's

RRR Wove Antique

made by P. H. Glatfelter Company.

It was printed and bound at

The Press of The World Publishing Company.

Typography and design are by

Lawrence S. Kamp